THEOLOGY OF THE DIACONATE

THEOLOGY OF THE DIACONATE
The State of the Question

The National Association of Diaconate Directors
Keynote Addresses, 2004

By
*Owen F. Cummings, William T. Ditewig,
and Richard R. Gaillardetz*

Paulist Press
New York/Mahwah, N.J.

Cover design by Cynthia Dunne
Book design by Lynn Else

Library of Congress Cataloging-in-Publication Data

Cummings, Owen F.
    Theology of the diaconate : the state of the question : the National Association of Diaconate Directors keynote addresses, 2004 / by Owen F. Cummings, William T. Ditewig, and Richard R. Gaillardetz.
        p.   cm.
    ISBN 0-8091-4345-3 (alk. paper)
    1. Deacons—Catholic Church. 2. Catholic Church—Doctrines. I. Ditewig, William T. II. Gaillardetz, Richard R., 1958–   III. Title.

BX1912.C865 2005
262'.142—dc22

                                                    2005001959

Published by Paulist Press
997 Macarthur Boulevard
Mahwah, New Jersey 07430

www.paulistpress.com

Printed and bound in the
United States of America

Contents

Publisher's Foreword

Father Lawrence Boadt, CSP

Book publishing usually reflects the dynamic direction of new thinking in religion and the church. As a subject becomes widely discussed and debated and theologians and church leaders begin to think about it more deeply, the number of publications grows rapidly. We are at such a moment now in the Catholic Church in the United States. The diaconate, as the authors in the following chapters demonstrate, is *not* new to the life of the church in our time, nor was it really lost or forgotten through the centuries. But the population explosion of the past century has caused the church to grow rapidly in membership, and the shortage of ordained priests to become more pronounced. This in turn has led to significant new emphasis on the way ministry functions for the church and has seen the emergence of significant new roles for the layperson ministering in the church and the broader context in which *ordained* ministry must be understood to fully include deacons working side by side with priests and bishops as fellow clergy.

Publisher's Foreword

The Paulist Press alone has published a great number of books related to the diaconate in recent years, and we especially welcome this new volume that explores the critical questions that must be addressed in order to build the solid foundations of a contemporary theology for the diaconate. The ancient order of deacon is being developed in new ways to meet the present needs of the church, and we are very pleased at Paulist Press to be able to provide this fine theological and spiritual overview of the task ahead by some of our most thoughtful and dynamic leaders in the diaconate today.

A Note of Introduction

Deacon Greg Urban

Executive Director
National Association of Diaconate Directors

Much has been written about the diaconate since the order was restored following Vatican II. Most texts deal with the diaconate the way it existed from the earliest days of the church. However, some theologians struggle with this early model. Why was the order of permanent diaconate reinstated? Was it primarily for deacons to help widows and orphans—to distribute food equitably at the proper time? Was it reinstated to fill a need due to a declining number of priests?

The answer to this question is more complex. Over the period of nearly the last three decades, deacons have proven invaluable in a wide variety of ministerial activities. Today's deacons, in increasing numbers, serve in administrative and other professional ministries of the church as well as the traditional liturgical, sacramental, and justice and peace areas. This new demand requires today's deacon to possess leadership as well as servant qualities. So what is a deacon really supposed to do? What did the church fathers intend at Vatican II? Have the job responsibilities of the deacon really changed from the church's earlier vision?

The National Association of Diaconate Directors (NADD), an organization at the forefront of Catholic diaconal studies, reviewed these questions at its annual convention held in Cherry Hill, NJ, during April 2004. We asked three well-known scholars—Deacon William T. Ditewig, PhD; Deacon Owen F. Cummings, MTh, DD; and Richard R. Gaillardetz, PhD—to address diaconal theology from three differing perspectives. Each presented a keynote address on this topic, and this book is an edited compilation of these talks.

I urge you to fasten your seat belts, for what follows is not at all conventional thinking. The authors discuss the state of the question today. This new thinking may challenge some, presenting ideas that may be ahead of their time. I encourage you to read it and dream—for the theology of the diaconate is still evolving.

Theology of the Diaconate: The State of the Question

Owen F. Cummings, PhD
Regents' Professor of Theology
Mount Angel Seminary

Fifteen years of ordained diaconal ministry as well as constant reading and thinking and teaching about the diaconate came together for me in my book *Deacons and the Church*.[1] That book offers a theological perspective on the diaconate from various angles: theology, history, spirituality, diaconal dysfunction, and so forth. In this essay my hope is to take up this theology of the diaconate and perhaps develop it a little more.

Introduction

Since 1967 the diaconate has been restored in many dioceses throughout the world, and in terms of both numbers

---

1. (New York/Mahwah, NJ: Paulist Press, 2004).

and of service to the church must be judged a huge success. In my judgment, however, success has not always marked attempts to articulate a compellingly persuasive theology of the diaconate. Some words of Cardinal Walter Kasper of the Vatican's Council for Promoting Christian Unity come to mind: "More than thirty years have passed since the Second Vatican Council, but much in the theological understanding of the ministry of the diaconate remains unclear and a matter of theological dispute, resulting in the variety of pastoral tasks assigned to deacons."[2] Kasper is making three claims here. First, the theology of the permanent diaconate remains unclear. Second, the theology of the permanent diaconate is a matter of dispute. Third, this unclarity and dispute result in the variety of pastoral tasks being assigned to deacons. This theological reflection will attempt to engage in a general way Cardinal Kasper's three points by analyzing some critical theological positions that have been taken recently on the diaconate, and by moving toward what might be called a pragmatic theology of the diaconate.

Critical Reflections on the Diaconate

Not every theologian or contributor to the question thinks that the restoration of the permanent diaconate has been a benefit to the church, or that the way the diaconate is pre-

---

2. Walter Kasper, "The Diaconate," in his *Leadership in the Church* (New York: The Crossroad Publishing Company, 2003), 13.

sently shaped and understood is a good thing. In this section I will review the positions of four authors in order to get a sense of the criticisms that are made of the permanent diaconate: Sherri Vallee, George Tavard, Basil Hume, and John N. Collins.

In a recent article on the diaconate, a Canadian liturgist, Sherri L. Vallee, makes the following comment: "The permanent diaconate, restored by Vatican II, is strongly promoted in some dioceses, while it continues to be avoided, minimized or overlooked in other dioceses. While some bishops actively encourage applicants to the permanent diaconate, others do not ordain permanent deacons for fear of creating unnecessary divisions between deacons and lay ministers."[3] This is but a statement of fact, reflecting the situation especially in North America, and the rather negative verbs used by Vallee are particularly striking—*avoided, minimized, overlooked.* So, while many dioceses—like my own Diocese of Salt Lake City—continue to promote the diaconate with gusto, a not insignificant number of Catholic priests and theologians are opposed to deacons. Their reasons vary, but two of the reasons one often hears are that the permanent diaconate is an impediment on the highway toward the ordination of women to the priesthood, and that it is an obstacle to the greater involvement of laity in the church. If this diaconal impediment is removed, the church will rapidly advance like so many other ecclesial traditions toward the recognition of

---

3. Sherri L. Vallee, "The Restoration of the Permanent Diaconate: A Blending of Roles," *Worship* 77 (2003): 530.

women as ordained ministers, it is alleged, or to the liberation of the laity. Leaving aside both the complex issue of the ordination of women in the Catholic Church and lay participation/ministry, this position seems to me ecclesiologically parsimonious. The advocates appear to suggest that, in order to enable women to serve and build up the church as priests, or laity to flourish in their baptismal calling to service, it is essential to disenfranchise a particular category of men from offering themselves as ministers to build up and serve the church, that is, deacons. While I have heard priests advocate the abandonment of the diaconate to clear the way for the priestly ordination of women or the increased service of laity, I have never heard them advocate the abandonment of priesthood to further the same causes. This kind of either/or thinking seldom is fruitful. What is needed is more both/and thinking about such critical issues.

One who does advocate the abandonment of the diaconate altogether in order to further the theology and practice of ministry in the church is the veteran Catholic ecumenical theologian, George H. Tavard. He seems to go further by suggesting that the diaconate's restoration was a false move and should simply now be abandoned. This abandonment would, he believes, force the church into a far freer and more creative thinking about the future shape of ministry. This is what Tavard had to say, writing in 1983:

Vatican Council II decided to restore a permanent diaconate, to be conferred on married as well as single men. This was clearly the start of an attempt at a minor restructuring of ministry. Yet this decision, I believe, was not very carefully weighed. For the problem of ministry does not reside in aligning future practice on ancient theory.... In keeping with Parkinson's law, superfluous work has to be created for the deacon. What a deacon is officially habilitated to perform can be done adequately by members of the laity. I would therefore suggest that the diaconate could be altogether abandoned, both in practice and in theory.... This might free us to think more creatively about future forms of ministry.[4]

One might react to Tavard in a number of ways. He speaks of "a minor restructuring of ministry." Though Tavard was writing over twenty years ago, he hugely underestimated the changes that have taken place in ministry. Many laypeople, both women and men, are involved as pastoral associates in very fruitful collaborative ministry throughout the continent. The enormous numerical success of the diaconate suggests more than a blip in contemporary ministry. In the United States, more than 13,000 permanent deacons are now serving, with a 50 percent increase over the past ten years.[5] Even

---

4. George H. Tavard, *A Theology for Ministry* (Wilmington, DE: Michael Glazier, 1983), 91.

5. Thomas Baker, "Two Cheers for Deacons," *Church* (Winter 2003): 14

if one comes at this numerical success through lenses other than the strictly theological—for example, sociological, cultural, even life-cycle changes—the theological lens and perception may not be dismissed if one espouses a Catholic ecclesiology. A Catholic ecclesiology accepts as foundational that the Spirit is at work in the church. What is the Spirit saying through the diaconate? Clearly, in view of both interest and numbers, something is being said! Ministry should not consist in realigning future practice on ancient theory, maintains Tavard. Who would disagree? And yet, ancient theory, the past of the living tradition that is the church today, can hardly be dismissed as irrelevant or redundant. One is tempted to ask what the abandonment of ancient theory would imply for the episcopate or the presbyterate. As for the idea that superfluous work has to be created for deacons, that may be true in some places, but it is certainly not the universal experience of deacons. Finally, Tavard says that the deacon performs tasks that may be done with at least equal adequacy by the laity. Here I believe that Tavard is on better theological ground, but where he sees this as an invitation to abandonment of the diaconate, I am inclined to see it as of the very essence of the diaconate. But more about that in the third and fourth parts of this essay.

The late archbishop of Westminster, Cardinal Basil Hume, was fond of saying that Pentecost is *now* and *always*, an ecclesiological principle that seems to me entirely accurate. And yet, in his beautiful little book, *Light in the Lord: Reflections on Priesthood*, there is no mention of deacons.[6] Perhaps one ought not expect any reflection on deacons in a book about the priesthood, but here is the table of contents in Cardinal Hume's book: Part One, Priests; Part Two, Bishops; Part Three, Laity. Maybe as a deacon I am being just a little oversensitive. I have heard it said, though I'd like to emphasize it is only hearsay, that Cardinal Hume had no time for deacons. He saw them as glorified altar servers and, to the best of my knowledge, ordained only one permanent deacon, a man who was a theologian in his diocese and personally requested ordination from his archbishop.

Let us return to the Canadian liturgist Sherri Vallee. She argues that historically and theologically two sets of functions may be described for the deacon. The first set of functions is traditionally associated with the diaconate in the New Testament and in the patristic period, and includes service in such forms as caring for the sick and elderly, visiting prisoners, and looking after the poor. "The church has a responsibility to look after the needs of society, and that service function has traditionally been embodied and symbolized in the role of the deacon."[7] Vallee adds pointedly, "These were roles of service, not roles of presidency."[8] The second set of functions consists of functions that are traditionally presbyteral or episcopal, but which have been assumed by deacons in recent times, for example, baptism, preaching, and

---

6. (Collegeville, MN: The Liturgical Press, 1991).
7. Sherri L. Vallee, op. cit., 531.
8. Ibid., 534.

presiding at weddings and funerals. The two sets of functions exercised by deacons create confusion, and the tensions and contradictions need to be addressed. Vallee argues that contemporary practices and roles of deacons blur important distinctions between priests and deacons. She continues:

> The Congregation for Catholic Education and the Congregation for Clergy appear to have decided on a view of the permanent diaconate that blurs the distinction between diaconate and presbyterate, that requires a very well-formed diaconate and that gives deacons many liturgical responsibilities that they did not have in the past. This decision represents a loss to the Church, because deacons in such functions cannot symbolize Christ as the humble servant in our midst. Moreover, when deacons baptize regularly, the connection between baptism and the Eucharist is obscured. When deacons preach at Mass, the connection between the Liturgy of the Word and the Liturgy of the Eucharist is less clear. Accentuation of a deacon's liturgical and sacramental responsibilities will undoubtedly lead to a further diminution of the church's attention to the social welfare needs of our communities.[9]

Much of what Vallee says here is theologically contestable. In summary, what she advocates seems to be a very close

---

9. Ibid., 552.

alignment of the contemporary and future diaconate with the past diaconate, and with the patristic past at that. This is not good historical or systematic ecclesiology. While there are definite and verifiable constants in the history of the church's ministry, there are also discontinuities, and all within a developing ecclesiology. Or, to cite again the late Cardinal Basil Hume, "Pentecost is now, and always." The Holy Spirit is animating the entire church today, and always has in the past, and always will in the future. This yields an understanding of tradition as the church continually perpetuating itself, animated by the Spirit, until the Parousia. The present determinations of the magisterium vis-à-vis the permanent diaconate surely may be understood as signals of the Spirit's continuing action—stimulating, enabling, prodding, promoting ministry in the church. Such ecclesiological considerations do not emerge with enough strength in the essay by Vallee. In her analysis of the present diaconate, there is too much focus on the *past* diaconate.

Finally, there is the work of the Australian Catholic scripture scholar, John N. Collins. "The first thing we hear about deacons in today's churches is that they are servants. Servants of Christ, servants of the church, servants of the people whose gathering makes up the church, servants in the margins of the world. Books about deacons attempt to be more precise about this."[10] This probably sounds good to the

---

10. John N. Collins, *Deacons and the Church: Making Connections Between Old and New* (Harrisburg, PA: Morehouse Publishing, 2002), 1.

diaconal community, but Collins believes that the emphasis on service, especially service to the needy and the marginal, is in fact not well founded. To provide a more well-founded grounding for the diaconate, there should be a return to the early church, but with qualification. Collins writes: "If we can come to a clearer understanding of early deacons we ought to be in a better position to decide what we ought to aim for in deacons for churches of our times. The search for a clearer understanding is not a search for an ancient model to which today's deacons would be expected to conform. Rather, the object of the search would be to clear away mis-understandings of the early deacons so that we would be able to avoid working from unreliable models."[11]

A most unreliable model, maintains Collins, is *diakonia* as service to the needy. This has become a dominant under-standing in contemporary theology, but a very questionable understanding for Collins, who notes that "[b]y the middle of the twentieth century this emphasis on understanding *diakonia* as service to the needy quickly began to have an impact on how ministry was generally understood in the church."[12] Collins traces the history of this theological mis-understanding in the twentieth century, beginning with *The Theological Dictionary of the New Testament*. The first German edition of this monumental work came out in 1935, and the English edition in 1965. There Wilhelm Brandt, who

---

11. Ibid., 2–3.
12. Ibid., 7.

was both a New Testament scholar and a chaplain to Lutheran deaconesses, provided the substantial article on diakonia. Collins writes about Brandt's article: "From this point onwards service as applied to the category within which the theology of ministry was to be constructed."[13] A good contemporary example, he maintains, is Thomas F. O'Meara's influential book, *Theology of Ministry,* published in 1983, with a second edition in 1999. O'Meara shows how a theology of service ought to be permeative in ministry. Another good example, this time specifically on the diaconate, emerged in James Monroe Barnett's widely used *The Diaconate: A Full and Equal Order,* first published in 1979, with a revised edition in 1995. This unhelpful service orientation is also found in the reception of *Lumen gentium* 29, where the permanent diaconate was restored to the Latin Church, "the ministry of the word, of the liturgy and of charity." Collins comments, "The last of these, however, is what receives most pastoral emphasis in teachings, in scholarly commentaries, and in pastoral training."[14] He points to the very large number of contributions in this regard in the American magazine for deacons, *Deacon Digest.* The emphasis is heaviest on charitable service. "While this emphasis remains dominant, over recent years some questioning has emerged as to the wisdom of focusing so strongly on service as the foundational element of the diaconate."[15]

---

13. Ibid., 8.
14. Ibid., 10.
15. Ibid., 12.

This questioning of diakonia as service has been the burden of Collins's own research. His 1990 book, *Diakonia: Reinterpreting the Ancient Sources,* examined in massive detail the linguistic and semantic fields of *diakonein* words in classical and Hellenistic Greek, as well as in the New Testament and early Christian sources. His conclusion is this: "Care, concern, and love—those elements of meaning introduced into the interpretation of this word and its cognates by Wilhelm Brandt—are just not part of their field of meaning."[16] The Lutheran ecumenical theologian, John Reumann, reviewing Collins's book in *The Patristic and Byzantine Review* (1991) considered the book's claim "devastating" for the theology of the diaconate, at least in his own Lutheran tradition. Private conversations with some participants at the 1995 International Diaconate Conference in Liverpool, England, confirms something of Reumann's "devastation." If service in terms of the diaconate is construed too narrowly, then Collins's strictures are well taken. But service in terms of building up the church that, in turn, is building up the world towards greater and more aware communion with God is what not only the diaconate but the church itself is all about. In my judgment it is this core concept of the church as communion that is the real deficiency in the positions at which we have looked.

---

16. (New York and Oxford: Oxford University Press, 1990), 254.

Owen F. Cummings

The Church as Communion

Any study of ministry must be rooted in ecclesiology, in a
theology of the church. In the years since the Second Vatican
Council, but with roots in the preconciliar traditions especially
of the nineteenth and twentieth centuries, we may observe a
shift from a juridical to other ways of doing ecclesiology. By
"juridical" in this context is meant an excessive emphasis on
the institutional dimension of the church, not an abjuration of
the institutional. In the English-speaking world we may point
to the enormous popularity of Cardinal Avery Dulles's *Models
of the Church,* which went into three editions, each subsequent
edition reflecting Dulles's further maturing perspective in theology. Dulles attempted to provide a cartography of the ecclesiological emphases and insights that were available in the
mid-1970s. His models were not to be understood as mutually
exclusive, but rather as a way of entering into the mystery of
the church, that excess of meaning and intelligibility that
inheres in the entire Christian body as church.

Today, *communion* is the preferred model of the church
in a variety of ways: as a hermeneutic lens for understanding
the cumulative ecclesiology of the documents of Vatican II,
as the preferred understanding of the church in the writings
of Pope John Paul II and of magisterial documents of the last
twenty years or so, and finally as the centrist approach to the
church in the World Council of Churches. Needless to say,
communion has a range of meanings in contemporary ecclesiology, finely laid out by Dennis Doyle in his book

Communion Ecclesiology.[17] Paraphrasing, but accurately, *Lumen gentium* 1, the church is a "sacrament of communion with God, and of communion among people." The church is a sign of communion and brings about communion, both with God and among people.

Arguably, the best, concrete representation of the church as communion is the annual Chrism Mass. Church is understood there not as a privilege nor a reward but a challenge and a task. It is a challenge to be a sacrament of communion in our too-fragmented and divided world, a world that lacks wholeness and health. "Vatican II said that the liturgy, especially the Eucharist, is the highest manifestation of the Church's true nature. This is emphatically the case with the Chrism Mass...."[18] The Chrism Mass is at the heart of this challenge of the church to be sacrament of communion for two reasons. First, in the ordinary course of the liturgical year the Chrism Mass is the one occasion in which the local church is most fully represented. At its center is the bishop. "The bishop...is a 'sacrament,' i.e., a visible and efficacious sign of Christ the High Priest.... Through [the bishop], the Christian people in the diocese have every sacrament: he consecrates the chrism, he ordains priests, every Eucharist is celebrated in communion with him.... This is what is mirrored in the Chrism Mass: the bishop, priests, deacons, [religious] and faithful of a local Church are gathered for the blessing of

---

17. (Maryknoll, NY: Orbis Books, 2000).
18. *Days of the Lord*, vol. 3 (Collegeville, MN: The Liturgical Press, 1993), 9.

14

the holy oils...."[19] The Chrism Mass is a powerful sacramental expression of the entire gathered church, the sacrament of communion with God and of communion among all the peoples of the earth.[20] The opening prayer prays:

> You anointed your only Son Messiah and Lord of
>   creation;
> You have given *us* a share in his consecration
> To priestly service in your Church.

The prayer implies that each and every one of us through baptism and confirmation is given to share in the consecration of Christ to priestly service, that we are called to be Christ the Priest. In the Preface we find the words:

> Christ gives the dignity of a royal priesthood
> To the people he has made his own.

There is no room for individualism here, but rather a mighty sense of being made one priestly people in Christ through God's sacramental action in the church. The priesthood of all the faithful and the ministerial priesthood share in the one priesthood of Christ, but differently. The whole tenor of the celebration of the Chrism Mass is to underscore our joint consecration to be a communion of witness and service in and to our world.

---

19. Ibid., 9–10.
20. My translation from *Lumen gentium* 1.

The second reason is this: In the Chrism Mass, we renew our vows—priests, deacons, religious, and laity. "We show God to the world" by making vows—of baptism, of celibacy, of poverty, of obedience—and by keeping them.[21] The fidelity, the day-to-day keeping of the promise or the vow points to and sacramentalizes God's fidelity to his creation, and especially to us. "It is one thing to say that one will give everything, offer all that one is now, and it is another to promise to go on year after year, no matter what happens."[22] God remains utterly faithful to us. The vows taken in baptism, in ordination, in religious life participate in that divine faithfulness and render visible to others the loving faithfulness that God is. The Chrism Mass is an ecclesial statement of the church's identity as communion, and a public statement and pledge to the world that our lives will be a visible portrayal of the infinite love God is and has for every human person. In an age that finds commitment until death extraordinarily difficult, the commitments in the Chrism Mass could not be more significant.

The oil of chrism invites Catholics to reaffirm as deeply and personally as possible our configuration to Christ through baptism, confirmation, and ordination. The oil of the sick invites Catholics to recognize our identity in illness and to con-join our sufferings to the One in whom we live and move and have our being. The oil of catechumens is

---

21. Timothy Radcliffe, OP, *I Have Called You Friends* (New York: Continuum, 2001), 90.

22. Ibid., 91–92.

intended to strengthen those among us who are making their way into the church, those who are preparing for incorporation, for embodiment in Christ. Thus, priests, deacons, religious, and all the faithful, including the sick and the elect—baptized and confirmed and ordained and about to be baptized and confirmed—are called each in her or his own way to be this chrismed presence of Christ in the world.

As church, we are not only the manifestation or showing forth of communion with God, but also an effective help in God's hand: the reality which, evangelized by God, evangelizes for God, and reconciled with God, reconciles with God, and drawn together by God, draws together for God.[23] The Chrism Mass gives us this primal sense and concrete expression of the church as communion. All are called to service-in-communion as church.

The Deacon as Servant-in-Communion

Cardinal Walter Kasper has been a staunch advocate of communion ecclesiology for many years now—undoubtedly connected to his Tübingen days as both student and professor and to the communion ecclesiology of the great nineteenth-century Tübingen scholar, Johann Adam Mohler—but in his most recently published *Leadership in the Church* he develops

---

23. Adapted from the late Jean M. R. Tillard, OP, as cited in Geoffrey Wainwright, "Roman Catholic-Methodist Dialogue: A Silver Jubilee," in Oliver Rafferty, SJ, ed., *Reconciliation: Essays in Honor of Michael Hurley* (Dublin: The Columba Press, 1993), 69.

aspects of this communion ecclesiology in relation to the diaconate. Kasper makes two key points from our perspective. First, this understanding of the church as communion shows that the church cannot be adequately understood as an end in itself, but must constantly be related to the kingdom of God. The church as communion is sacrament of this kingdom, both signing it forth and promoting its development. This is how Kasper puts it: "The church is seen to exist, not for its own sake but for others: for human beings, for a world in need of unity, reconciliation and peace. The church is a servant church. In its broadest sense, then, *diaconia* is not just one dimension of the church: it is its essential dimension."[24] Second, as Vatican II noted, the fullness of orders, that is, the fullness of the sacramental representation of Christ, resides in the bishop. According to Kasper, "Deacons and priests have their own specific gradated participation in the one sacramental office that the bishop possesses in fullness; the council sees them as collaborators of the bishop, dependent on him and subordinate to him. Their ministry is to represent the bishop, who needs collaborators and helpers because of the sheer volume of work that is expected of him.... The bishop is aided by two separate arms, so to speak, which have differing tasks but must collaborate with one another."[25] Though he does not allude to it, Kasper could have been describing the Chrism Mass.

---

24. Walter Kasper, op. cit., 25.
25. Ibid., 17–18.

Theologically and ecclesiologically, then, there is no competition among deacon, priest, and bishop. Deacons and priests participate in the fullness of orders that is the episcopate. Nor is there any competition between ordained ministry and what has come to be known as lay ministry. Both are necessary for the building up of the church, as sacrament of communion. Richard Gaillardetz expresses it comprehensively when he says, "There is no competition in the life of public service on behalf of the church. Lectors, eucharistic ministers, ministers of hospitality, deacons, priests and bishops—these ministries do not compete with one another in the liturgy but cooperate in a wonderful way to build up the body of Christ at worship."[26] How could there be competition when the very raison d'être of the *entire* church as communion is to collaborate in signifying communion and in promoting communion?

For such reasons as these, Cardinal Kasper writes, "In a special manner, [the deacon] is to represent the specifically diaconal dimension of *all* church ministry, i.e., the servant-ministry of Jesus Christ in the church."[27] This service-in-communion of the deacon, says Kasper, must be understood "in a comprehensive theological and ecclesiological sense as including the ministry of proclamation and service at the altar, as well as leadership tasks.... When we speak of the ministry of the deacon from the perspective of *diaconia,* we

---

26. Richard Gaillardetz, "Vatican II's Liturgy Constitution: The Beginnings of a Liturgical Ecclesiology," *Origins* (October 30, 2003): 351.

27. Walter Kasper, op. cit., 21.

must include all three basic dimensions of ecclesial ministry, *martyria,* and *liturgia* as well as *diaconia* in the narrower sense of the word."[28] Kasper means by *martyria, liturgia,* and *diaconia* what *Lumen gentium* 29 and postconciliar documentation understand as "ministry of the word, sacrament, and charity." By putting himself at the disposal of the bishop for ministry to the word, sacrament, and charity, in accordance with his gifts and aptitudes and the ecclesial discernment of the bishop, the deacon's visible and verifiable service-in-communion is intended to draw forth service-in-communion in the church as a whole.

Let's interpret "ministry of the word" to mean intellectual service: understanding and interpreting and proclaiming the holy scriptures, engaging in the theological disciplines both personally and professionally as in the Rite for the Christian Initiation of Adults, adult faith formation, directing retreats, preaching, and so forth. Each of these forms of service has to do with the intellectual dimension of the church understood broadly.

Let's interpret "ministry of sacrament" to mean mystical service: literally serving as a liturgical minister at the altar during the Eucharist—the very center of all sacramental and liturgical service; the commitment to the Liturgy of the Hours on behalf of the whole church; the discipline of regular prayer and meditation in one's own life, which is always corporate and never individual; the ministry of mystagogy, that is, leading

---

28. Ibid., 21–22.

others to the mystery of encounter and communion with God, again always corporate and never individual. Each form of service has to do with the mystical dimension of the church understood broadly.

Let's interpret "ministry of charity" to mean institutional service: administration, various kinds of service such as prison ministry, ministry to the sick, ministry to the grieving, to those preparing for marriage, and so forth. Each ministry has to do with the institutional dimension of the church understood broadly.

In point of fact, these three shapes of the diaconate as envisaged in *Lumen gentium* 29—ministry of word, sacrament, and charity—encapsulate how the diaconate has been practiced and understood throughout the tradition, and not just in the patristic period that tends to be privileged above all else. Some actual examples will help to put flesh on these bones of word, sacrament, and charity.

For the patristic period, think of Lawrence of Rome and Ephrem of Nisibis. Lawrence was one of the seven deacons at Rome under the pontificate of Pope Sixtus II. He was probably put to death under the emperor Valerian in 258, just four days after the martyrdom of Pope Sixtus II and his four deacons. Lawrence probably was beheaded, though, according to the received tradition, he was put to death, roasted on a gridiron.[29] After the Edict of Toleration, the

---

29. For example, see Michael P. McHugh, "Lawrence," in Everett Ferguson, ed., *Encyclopedia of Early Christianity*, 2nd ed., vol. 2 (New York and London: Garland Publishing Company, 1997), 668.

emperor Constantine, about 330, had a church and later a large basilica built above Lawrence's tomb. These buildings demonstrate Lawrence's popularity with Roman Christians. "In fact, no saint, except Saints Peter and Paul, was more honored by the people of Rome from the time of Constantine on."[30] According to the testimony of St. Ambrose of Milan, the prefect of Rome asked Lawrence to reveal the whereabouts of the treasures of the church. So, Lawrence brought together the poor and the sick and said, "These are the treasures of the church." The poor, and indeed all the people, are the treasures of the church because, in Lawrence's terms, Christ lives in them. Christ lives in them because, according to Matthew 25:31–46, Christ is identified with the hungry, the thirsty, the poor. Lawrence had as one of his roles the dispensing of alms to those Christians in need. The deacon was the steward who knew the poor well and who looked after them. Lawrence was primarily a *minister of charity.*

Ephrem of Nisibis (ca. 306–373) was a Syrian deacon who ministered in the ancient cities of Nisibis and Edessa. He established a school of biblical and theological studies. He composed hymns, homilies, and commentaries on holy scripture. Many of his writings had an explicitly liturgical setting. We are told by St. Jerome that in some churches Ephrem's compositions were recited after the scriptural les-

---

30. Vincent L. Kennedy, *The Saints of the Canon of the Mass,* 2nd ed. (Città del Vaticano: Pontificio Istituto di Archeologia Cristiana, 1963), 134.

sons in the liturgy.[31] Ephrem wrote theology in the form of poetry, in Syriac, a dialect of Aramaic, very close to the language our Lord himself spoke. He has been considered "the greatest poet of the patristic age, and perhaps the only theologian-poet to rank beside Dante."[32] Ephrem was primarily a *minister of the word,* though he died ministering to those suffering from the plague in Edessa.

For the medieval period think of Alcuin of York and Francis of Assisi. Alcuin of York was the deacon brought by Charlemagne to his capital city of Aachen to be master of the school. Charlemagne undertook a great renaissance of learning throughout his Frankish Kingdom, and the architect of this renewal was the deacon Alcuin. He was involved in formal teaching of philosophy and theology. He was also involved in the practicalities of the liturgical renewal of his day, again initiated by Charlemagne. We might say that Alcuin was a *minister of the word* and of *sacrament* and of *charity.*

Of Francis of Assisi (1181–1226) Bishop Mark Santer writes, "Of all the saints, the one whom most people find most Christlike is St. Francis. And I think it is significant that he was

---

31. Sidney H. Griffith, ST, "Ephraem: The Deacon of Edessa, and the Church of the Empire," in Thomas P. Halton and Joseph P. Williman, eds., *Diakonia, Studies in Honor of Robert T. Meyer* (Washington, DC: The Catholic University of America Press, 1986), 22–52, and "A Spiritual Father for the Whole Church, St. Ephraem the Syrian," *Sobornost* 20 (1998): 27. See also Paul S. Russell, "St. Ephraem, the Syrian Theologian," *Pro Ecclesia* 7 (1998): 82.

32. Robert Murray, SJ, *Symbols of Church and Kingdom: A Study in Early Syriac Tradition* (Cambridge: Cambridge University Press, 1975), 31.

never a priest. He was ordained deacon, a servant, to the end of his life."[33] Our emphasis will be to view Deacon Francis's entire life and ministry as diaconal, and in particular, his love for God's creation. Francis's poverty and holy folly brought about in him what can only be called an "inner freedom," a freedom in which there was no stress, no anxiety because he had cast his cares on the Lord and trusted in him with a joyous abandonment. "The fundamental truth about this simple but fascinating human being is that he was completely filled with God."[34] When you are filled with the truth that is God, you will look strange to other people, as John Saward has it: "In a world gone mad the guardian of truth is invariably dismissed as a raving lunatic."[35] Francis's love for God's creation finds a fine summary in the words of Louis K. Dupré: "Who in thirteenth century Italy had a deeper impact upon his culture than Francis of Assisi, an uneducated man, of average intelligence, but a visionary who saw all creation filled with divine life? After him we looked with different eyes at nature, animals, people. We wrote different poetry and we fashioned different paintings. We lived and loved differently."[36] This is no

---

33. Mark Santer, "Diaconate and Discipleship," *Theology* 81 (1978): 181.

34. Duane V. Lapsanski, "Francis of Assisi: An Approach to Franciscan Spirituality," in E. Rozanne Elder, ed., *The Spirituality of Western Christendom* (Kalamazoo, MI: Cistercian Publications, 1976), 121.

35. Op. cit., 1.

36. *The Deeper Life: An Introduction to Christian Mysticism* (New York: Crossroad, 1981), 55.

sentimentalism on Dupré's part, but a judgment that could be amply verified historically. Nature poetry, but in relation to God, comes into its own after Francis. In terms of painting, one thinks of the frescoes of Giotto, which had a huge influence on European painting. Behind these developments, as Dupré says, lies Francis himself, a man in love with God and with all God's creation. One of Francis's prayers was the short ejaculation, "My God and all things!" To love God is to love God's creation. "When one gives oneself to God, all creation is drawn along."[37] It is out of this deep conjunction of God and creation that Francis was able to pen the canticle "Brother Sun," hymning God's praise through all God's creatures, great and small. It is the central Catholic sacramental imagination at work, responding to God's presence everywhere. Francis's diaconate may be seen as a ministry of *word* and *sacrament,* inviting people to a closer sense of God's communion with them.

For the Reformation period, think of Reginald Pole and Nicholas Ferrar. The sixteenth and early seventeenth centuries are extremely complex, and the treatment of both Pole and Ferrar will simply be to illustrate the diversity of diaconal service. Reginald Pole, a relative of King Henry VIII of England, had an excellent education, and was ordained deacon. It was only in the last year or so of his life that Pole was

---

37. Anton Rotzetter, OFM Cap, "The Basic Experience," in Anton Rotzetter, OFM Cap, Willibrord-Christian Van Dijk, OFM Cap, and Thadee Matura, OFM, *Gospel Living: Francis of Assisi Yesterday and Today* (New York: St. Bonaventure University–The Franciscan Institute, 1994), 116.

ordained priest and bishop, and so we may rightly claim him as a deacon. Pole spent much of his life in theology and in church administration. For example, he was the papal legate at the opening session of the reforming Council of Trent. He got into some difficulty because he was more open ecumenically than others, recognizing some theological insight on the part of the Reformers. So, here is a deacon who serves the church through careful and informed administration and theology. We might say Pole's was a *ministry of the word* and of *charity*.

Nicholas Ferrar (1592–1637) was an Anglican deacon.[38] In the words of Mark Santer: "Nicholas Ferrar was ordained deacon so as to be able to lead his household's prayers and to be consecrated to the service of his Lord. But he would not be a priest."[39] After education at the University of Cambridge and travels abroad, in 1625 Ferrar settled at Little Gidding, an estate in Huntingdonshire. Members of his family joined him there and established a sort of religious community. The community numbered about thirty in all. He was ordained a deacon by William Laud, then bishop of St. David's, in Westminster Abbey on Trinity Sunday, 1626. The Little Gidding community, under Ferrar's leadership and guid-

---

38. See the brief biography by Mandell Creighton, "Ferrar, Nicholas," in *The Dictionary of National Biography,* vol. 6 (Oxford: Oxford University Press, original publication date 1889, reprinted 1921–22), 1241–44.

39. Mark Santer, op. cit., 181.

ance, lived a life of devout prayer and worked under a strict rule from 1625 until 1646.[40] The entire Psalter was recited every day and the gospels once a month. As well as this, two members kept religious vigil every night from 9:00 p.m. until 1:00 a.m. As well as their life of prayer, the Little Gidding community was involved in charitable work for the benefit of the whole neighborhood: the distribution of food for the poor, visiting both the poor and the sick, running a free dispensary for the needy, and offering schooling for the children of the local village. Ferrar's own life has been described as "a perpetual prayer."[41] We can truly say that Deacon Ferrar was a *minister of the word* and of *charity*.

What may be observed through these examples from the patristic, medieval, and Reformation periods is that there is little uniformity in the service-in-communion of deacons down through the ages. Much depended upon their gifts, how the church used them, and what the church asked of them. We may conclude that if a historical perspective is taken, there simply is no one mold into which every deacon has to fit. What he has to fit, as it were, is this wholehearted commitment to service-in-communion.

---

40. "Little Gidding," in Frank L. Cross and Elizabeth A. Livingstone, eds., *The Oxford Dictionary of the Christian Church,* 2nd ed. (Oxford: Oxford University Press, 1973), 828.

41. Ibid., 190.

Conclusion

Sherri Vallee concludes in her recent essay that presidential/liturgical roles for deacons arise "primarily for pragmatic reasons," that is, the shortage of priests.[42] There may be some level at which that is true. However, it is being suggested in this presentation that the great upsurge of interest in the diaconate in our times is the way the Spirit is shaping ministry in the church toward the future. No one knows precisely the shape of ministry in the future. Guesses are just that: guesses! What is not a guess and what is not speculation is that at this time, *here and now,* deacons are being called to service-in-communion in a variety of ways, and historically that seems to have been the pattern in the church. There never was only one way to serve as a deacon.

Walter Kasper describes the diaconate in these terms: "This 'downwardly mobile career' is described in the christological hymn in the Letter to the Philippians (2: 6–11), which prescribes the basic Christian virtue, as the spiritual tradition teaches, namely the attitude of humility, which is a willingness to serve. This must be *a fortiori* the basic attitude of the deacon."[43] Kasper seems to be saying, as this presentation is claiming, that there is no one way to be a deacon, but every way must be identifiable and recognizable as *a form of service,* inviting and empowering

---

42. Op. cit., 543.
43. Op. cit., 39.

others to serve in such a way that communion with God and communion among people is advanced. That is pragmatically what it means to be church and what it means to be a deacon in the church.

Charting a Theology of Diaconate: An Exercise in Ecclesial Cartography

William T. Ditewig, PhD

Executive Director
Secretariat for the Diaconate
United States Conference of Catholic Bishops

Introduction: Theology and the Diaconate

The challenges faced when attempting to devise a coherent theology of the diaconate remind me of the famous PhD comprehensive examination question that demands: "Describe the history of the papacy from its origins to the present day; concentrate especially but not exclusively on the social, political, economic, religious, and philosophical impact on Europe, Asia, the Americas, and Africa. Be brief, concise, and specific." Nonetheless, however difficult the task, the need to develop theologies of the

31

diaconate remains no less necessary, even critical, at this point in time in the life of the church.

This presentation is in two sections of unequal lengths. Following a brief introduction, the main body will consider ten points of reference toward a theology of the diaconate that is true to our scriptural, historical, and conciliar roots while responding positively to the challenges and opportunities of the contemporary church.

Perhaps the biggest challenge to face, however, is the simple fact that comprehensive, systematic theological discourse on the diaconate has rarely, if ever, been done. Given the history of the diaconate and its potential as a renewed order, this is somewhat surprising. Consider the vision of one theologian on the eve of the council, Dom Augustinus Kerkvoorde, OSB. Born in Belgium in 1913, he joined the Benedictines in 1932 and was ordained a priest in 1939. After earning a doctorate in theology from Louvain in 1943, Kerkvoorde wrote extensively on sacramental theology and eucharistic spirituality. Like Karl Rahner and others, he became interested in the possibilities of a renewed diaconate shortly after the Second World War. In 1962, Karl Rahner invited Dom Augustinus to contribute to the major text he was editing on the diaconate, *Diaconia in Christo*.

In his article, Kerkvoorde observed that a theology of the diaconate had not been needed in the past since the diaconate had been for more than a millennium more of a "theoretical" function on the road to the priesthood and, as such, didn't "arouse a demand for a thoroughly elaborated dogma about the diaconate."[1] However, he forecast a change if the council renewed the diaconate:

> Once it becomes apparent that this rank may be revived in the near term, such theologies will undoubtedly spring up like mushrooms....There will be plenty of authors and publishers who will routinely pounce on this unexpected inheritance. If by that time theology has not succeeded in setting up some clear and simple principles for the restoration of the diaconate, and if its deepest meaning has not been made visible for both the learned and for the simple faithful, then this ancient and divinely established institution will easily soon be in danger of going down the same path as many other ecclesiastical institutions. The diaconate, which should take its normal place in the Church as an institution that will bring both balance and vitality, runs the risk of becoming a superfluous organ, smothered and frustrated— that is, if it is not first choked to death in the literature and in controversy before it can even be reborn.[2]

1. Augustinus Kerkvoorde, OSB, "Theology of the Diaconate," in *Foundations for the Renewal of the Diaconate* (Washington, DC: USCC, 1993, reissued in 2003), 91.
2. Ibid., 92.

One might wish that Kerkvoorde's vision of significant theological activity on the diaconate would have been realized. Certainly there have been major contributions to diaconal theology,[3] but they have certainly not "sprung up like mushrooms," nor have many authors "pounced upon this unexpected inheritance"! Nonetheless, Kerkvoorde's caution was well-founded that if the deepest meaning of a renewed diaconate were not made "visible" for "the learned and the simple," then the diaconate as a permanent order would soon become superfluous, smothered, and frustrated. His vision that the diaconate could be an order of "vitality and balance" seems even more appealing in today's world.

---

3. See, for example, James M. Barnett, *The Diaconate: A Full and Equal Order,* rev. ed. (Valley Forge, PA: Trinity Press International, 1995); Piercarlo Beltrando, *Diaconi per la Chiesa* (Milano: Instituto Propaganda, 1977); Alphonse Borras and Bernard Pottier, *Le grâce du diaconat: Questions actuelles autour du diaconat latin* (Brussels: Editions Lessius, 1998); Norbert Brockman, *Ordained to Service: A Theology of the Permanent Diaconate* (Hicksville, NY: Exposition Press, 1976); Leo M. Croghan, "The Theology and the Spirit of the Diaconate's Restoration," in *American Ecclesiastical Review* 161 (1969): 293–301; Edward P. Echlin, SJ, *The Deacon in the Church: Past and Future* (Staten Island, NY: Alba House, Society of St. Paul, 1971); Josef Hornef, "The Order of Diaconate in the Roman Catholic Church," trans., Patrick Russell, in *The Diaconate Now,* ed. Richard T. Nolan, 57–79 (Washington, DC: Corpus, 1968); Josef Hornef, "The Genesis and Growth of the Proposal," in *Foundations for the Renewal of the Diaconate,* Bishops' Committee on the Permanent Diaconate, 5–27 (Washington, DC: United States Catholic Conference, 1993); Joseph A. Komonchak, "The Permanent Diaconate and the Variety of Ministries in the Church," in *Diaconal Quarterly* III/3 (1977): 15–23; III/4 (1977): 29–40; IV/1 (1978): 13–25; Karl Rahner and Herbert Vorgrimler, eds., *Diakonia in Christo: Über Die Erneuerung des Diakonates* (Freiburg: Herder, 1962).

Nearly thirty-five years after Kerkvoorde's challenge, the Bishops' Committee on the Diaconate in 1996 released the results of a national study on the diaconate in which they identified seven "Issues for the Future."[4] The very first of these posed the following question: "How are the issues of the deacon's identity and acceptance to be resolved in light of the tendency of many to use the deacon to address the present shortage of priests?"[5] Another issue is closely related to the first: "What are the best means of response to the demonstrated need for a more focused effort on the national and diocesan levels to form and challenge deacons toward roles and ministries more clearly differentiated from the ministerial priesthood?"[6] The bishops conclude, "The challenge of the next decades will be to make these developments more theologically rich and thus to expand the deacon's sense of ministry, evangelization, and service continually, even beyond the parish."[7] While there is certainly much more than theology packed into these questions, theology is a necessary partner in the conversations demanded to address these and so many other related issues.

---

4. United States Catholic Conference, *A National Study on the Permanent Diaconate of the Catholic Church in the United States: 1994–1995* (Washington, DC: USCC, 1996).

5. Ibid., 15.

6. Ibid.

7. Ibid., 16.

Plotting a Course: Ten Points of Reference

The 1998 *Basic Norms for the Formation of Permanent Deacon* (BNFPD) correctly asserts that "the effectiveness of the formation of permanent deacons depends to a great extent on the theological understanding of the diaconate that underlies it."[8] This theological understanding "offers the co-ordinates for establishing and guiding the formation process and, at the same time, lays down the end to be attained."[9] However, the document goes on to acknowledge that "the almost total disappearance of the permanent diaconate from the Church of the West for more than a millennium has certainly made it more difficult to understand the profound reality of this ministry."[10] It continues that there are nonetheless certain "authoritative points of reference," and proceeds to identify six of them,[11] acknowledging that these are not the only points of reference and that even these will need to be "developed and deepened."[12] Daring to go "where angels might fear to tread" (to quote Alexander Pope), I now propose ten points of reference that might contribute toward this development and deepening.

---

8. Congregation for Catholic Education, *Basic Norms for the Formation of Permanent Deacons* (Vatican City: Libreria Editrice Vaticana, 1998), #3.

9. Ibid.

10. Ibid.

11. Ibid., #3, with the "authoritative points of reference" being presented in #4–#8.

12. Ibid.

Point #1: *A proper theological understanding of the diaconate presumes a "new way of thinking" about the sacramental nature of the church and its ordering of ministry.*

When I was a commander in the navy, one of the first things I learned is the necessary plotting of a course by selection of the right charts of the seas being sailed. Consider the various types of projections we use in our maps and charts: Mercator, Robinson, Polar, the Albers Equal Area, the Lambert Conformal Conic, the Mollweide, Orthographic, Gnomonic, and so many others. Why are so many needed? The reasons are simple and basic: to enhance accuracy and to avoid distortion. Those must also be the goals of the theologian: to enhance accuracy and avoid distortion.

Just as different map projections force us to look at the same piece of the earth or ocean in a new way, what is needed for a theology of ministry is a new way of thinking. Both Paul VI and John Paul II have spoken of the *novus mentis habitus* (a new way of thinking) reflected in the discussions and documents of the Second Vatican Council. For example, during the preparation of the 1983 Code of Canon Law, Paul VI reminded the Code Commission that this new way of thinking provided by the council was to be reflected not only in the practical applications of the law but in the very structures and processes of the code itself. In promulgating the finished product, John Paul II reaffirmed that what is new in the new code is more than a few practical adjustments; it is the newness of Vatican II itself.[13]

As is well known, of course, critical components of the council's new way of thinking involved the way we describe the very nature and mission of the church herself. This is illustrated through any number of examples from the council and its documents. However, one particular event at the council seems to illustrate this vision quite powerfully and succinctly. On December 7, 1965, the day before the solemn closing of the Second Vatican Council in St. Peter's Square, the council fathers celebrated Mass together with Pope Paul VI in St. Peter's Basilica. In this fraternal setting, the pope offered his own reflection on the ultimate significance of the council's work in these words:

> We stress that the teaching of the Council is channeled in one direction, the service of humankind, of every condition, in every weakness and need. The Church has declared herself a servant of humanity at the very time when her teaching role and her pastoral government have, by reason of this Church solemnity, assumed greater splendor and vigor. However, the idea of service has been central.[14]

---

13. James H. Provost, "Canonical Reflection on Selected Issues in Diocesan Governance," in *The Ministry of Governance,* James K. Mallet, ed. (Washington, DC: CLSA, 1986), 211, citing Paul VI, Allocution to Code Commission, November 20, 1965: *AAS* 57 (1965): 988.

14. Paul VI, *Hodie concilium, AAS* 58 (1966): 57–64.

In short, the "new way of thinking" proposed by the council is reflected in a servant-ecclesiology. This servant-ecclesiology, then, becomes the proper "chart" on which to plot the course for a diaconal theology. It permits a new way of thinking about many things: about the meaning of sacramental initiation; about the resulting nature of ministry in general and ordained ministry in particular; about the multifaceted and multidimensional relationships that are involved in lives of Christian discipleship; about the nuances that exist within the sacrament of orders itself. Several contemporary theologians, including Dr. Richard Gaillardetz, have called for a renewed effort at finding new ways to relate commissioned, installed, appointed, and ordained ministries. This creative approach reflects the challenge of not putting new wine into old wineskins (Luke 5:37), and a similar new way of thinking will now inform each of the following points.

Point #2: The diaconate is part of the mystery of the church as trinitarian communion in missionary tension.

Using a phrase first found in *Pastores dabo vobis*, the 1998 *Basic Norms for the Formation of Permanent Deacons* cites as an essential theological reference point the fact that "we must consider the diaconate, like every other Christian identity, from within the Church which is understood as a mystery of Trinitarian communion in missionary tension." The church as a mystery of trinitarian communion: A recent Internet search for the phrase "trinitarian communion" revealed a staggering 534 instances, most of which refer back to a variety of church and papal documents. Pope John Paul II is fond of saying that the trinitarian communion is "model," "reference," and "archetype" of ecclesial communion. One theologian has captured this relationship briefly but well when she writes:

> Our baptism into the paschal mystery of Jesus immerses us into a God who is not the poverty of aloneness, God as an isolated individual, but God as the richness of trinitarian communion. Nowhere else is there such absolute oneness and yet such utterly unique personhood. Nowhere else does the mystery of human persons called to both autonomy and communion find its source and goal than in the infinite uniqueness and communion of the persons who are God. And precisely in not running away from the price of our own personhood we begin to discover that the proclamations central to the Christian message are not simply doctrines to be believed, but reality that can be experienced, reality that can transform experience.[15]

Theologies of diaconate—as indeed all theology—must begin with a full appreciation of the power, risk, and mystery of sacramental initiation into the Trinity. This provides a

---

15. Mary Ann Fatula, OP, "Autonomy and Communion: Paying the Price," *Spirituality Today,* vol. 39 (Summer 1987): 164.

common sacramental identity while establishing the possibilities for creative, dynamic, Spirit-filled, and transformative mission. Categories of theological discourse that insist upon excessive distinctions between "the baptized" over against "the ordained" will benefit from dialogue with trinitarian theology as the archetype of all ecclesial ministry. Furthermore, ongoing intensive research into the relationship of sacramental initiation to the varieties of commissioned, installed, instituted, and ordained ministries must be encouraged.

The profound implications of sacramental initiation and trinitarian communion on the categories of contemporary ministries, which of course includes the diaconate, need further development. The second phrase of this set of coordinates—much as longitude is to latitude—that this trinitarian communion is lived "in missionary tension," gives communion a vector, a direction, a goal: in short, a mission. In many ways, the points that follow are all attempts at describing facets of this mission. But as part of our new way of thinking, perhaps we can take a powerful insight from Cardinal Roger Mahony of Los Angeles. In a recent address to the Eucharistic Congress held in the Diocese of El Paso, Texas, he shared his conviction that "it is not so much that the church has a mission; it is rather more that the mission has a church."

> What is this mission? It is none other than that of Jesus, Christ, the Word, and of the Holy Spirit, the gift of God's love dwelling in our hearts. Jesus' mission is to announce the time of God's favor, the

coming of the reign of God. Jesus proclaimed the reign of God as the fulfillment of God's hope, desire and intention for the world now and to come. In God's reign, truth, holiness, justice, love and peace will hold sway forever. Jesus established the church to continue and further this mission.... This mission is so central to the word and work of Jesus that the Second Vatican Council affirmed and emphasized that *mission* defines the church. The church in every dimension of its life and practice exists for mission: to proclaim in word and deed the reign of God to people in every culture, time and place.[16]

The mission of the church is shared by all in communion; the participation of one ordained into the order of deacons is collaborative and collegial, one which speaks the words of Christ in his name and in the name of the church. The deacon acts as a minister ordered in the Spirit by his bishop, an instrument of Christ and of the church Christ established to carry on his mission.

Point #3: The christological dimension of diaconate is expressive of the kenosis of God.

John Paul II has written that "the prime commitment of theology is seen to be the understanding of God's *kenosis*, a

---

16. Cardinal Roger Mahony, "Church of the Eucharist, a Communion for Mission," in *Origins* 33:42 (April 1, 2004): 723.

grand and mysterious truth for the human mind, which finds it inconceivable that suffering and death can express a love which gives itself and seeks nothing in return."[17] While much of the literature that has developed on the nature of the ordained ministry has focused on the priesthood, very little has been done to address the nature of an ordained ministry that is *not* sacerdotal. This means that existing categories of theological discourse must be carefully critiqued to determine their applicability to the diaconate.

While the sacerdotal orders often speak of their relationship to the priesthood of Christ, it seems to me that a possibility for a particularly diaconal language might be found in the notion of kenosis itself, as found for example in the famous hymn in Philippians, in which we hear that Christ "emptied himself, taking the form of a slave, being born in human likeness," and even accepting death on a cross (Phil 2:6–11). It is in this very act of pouring himself out that resulted in Christ's exaltation. This counterintuitive path of emptying to exaltation becomes the very path for Christ's disciples to follow.[18]

---

17. John Paul II, *Fides et ratio* (Vatican City: Vatican Polyglot Press, 1998), #93.

18. Christ's kenotic path to glory as found in Philippians 2:6–11 is described by Walter Kasper as a "downwardly mobile career...which prescribes the basic Christian virtue, as the spiritual tradition teaches, namely, the attitude of humility, which is a willingness to serve. This must *a fortiori* be the basic attitude of the deacon." Walter Kasper, *Leadership in the Church: How Traditional Roles Can Serve the Christian Community Today* (New York: Crossroad, 2003), 39.

Christ's own kenosis is of course a part of each Christian's life, and in the life of the Christian community. Jean Corbon speaks of two kenoses when he writes, "Having become the Church, we must live the Church's life as a *kenosis* of the Spirit. The gift to us of God's ever faithful love must be answered by an authentic life of charity which the Holy Spirit pours into our hearts. We too must give our gift fully; that is, we must divest ourselves of ourselves in that same *kenosis* of love...."[19]

Ordination to any order celebrates a sacramental empowerment of the church. The church is empowered by the Spirit with the particular gifts of the ordinand now being placed at the permanent and public service of the church herself. Through ordination the deacon is likewise empowered, not with the *sacra potestas* often associated with the sacerdotal orders of bishops and presbyters, but with a *kenotic power,* a power or strength to empty himself in service to the church through his participation in the apostolic ministry of the bishop.

The linkage between the apostles' exercise of authority and kenotic self-sacrifice in imitation of Christ is found in several places in the New Testament. For purposes of illustration, we shall consider Christ's washing the disciples' feet in the Gospel of John. During his homily during 2004's Mass of the Lord's Supper, Pope John Paul II pointed out that

---

19. Jean Corbon, *The Wellspring of Worship* (New York/Mahwah, NJ: Paulist Press, 1988), 106–7, cited in Michael Downey, "Theology as a Way of Life," *New Theology Review* 15:1 (February 2002): 60.

Jesus, in washing the feet of the apostles, performed an act "that normally would be done by a servant, thus wishing to impress on the minds of the Apostles the meaning of what would shortly happen. In fact, the passion and death are the fundamental service of love by which the Son of God freed humankind from sin."[20] The implication of this passage for the identity and ministry of the apostles is profound, since it links the kenotic self-sacrifice of Christ to the life of the disciple. "To 'have part with Jesus' through washing means to be part of the self-giving love that will bring Jesus' life to an end, symbolically anticipated by the foot washing."[21]

Furthermore, those who would be leaders in the community of disciples are to be identified by their own self-sacrificing love in imitation of the kenosis of Christ:

> The theme of death is behind the use of the word *hypodeigma* [v. 15]. This expression, found only here in the N[ew] T[estament]...is associated with exemplary death. Jesus' exhortation is not to moral performance but to imitation of his self-gift....Entrance into the Johannine community of disciples meant taking the risk of accepting the *hypodeigma* of Jesus, a commitment to love even if it led to death.[22]

---

20. John Paul II, Homily at the Mass of the Lord's Supper, 2004. Reported in Vatican Information Service 040414, N. 67, April 14, 2004.

21. Francis J. Moloney, *The Gospel of John* (Collegeville, MN: The Liturgical Press, 1998), 375.

22. Ibid., 376.

The *Directory for the Ministry and Life of Permanent Deacons* concludes: "The primary and most fundamental relationship [of the deacon] must be with Christ, who assumed the condition of a slave for love of the Father and mankind. In virtue of ordination the deacon is truly called to act in conformity with Christ the Servant."[23]

Kenotic power is not the exclusive province of the deacon, but it is the deacon who serves as the sacramental focus for the *diakonia* of the entire community. That is why McCaslin and Lawler can say, "A parish, which is a local incarnation of Church and of Jesus, is not sacramentally whole if it is without either priest or deacon."[24] Just as the presbyter shares in the sacred power of the priesthood with the bishop, so too does the deacon share in the kenotic power of the diaconate with the bishop.

The challenge for the contemporary diaconate is to realize the ramifications of this kenosis, a totally self-sacrificial strength for service. In real terms this means that deacons must divorce themselves from any expressions, attitudes, and behaviors that smack of clericalism or the acquisition of power and authority for its own sake. This means that there should be something unique in the ways in which deacons serve that demonstrates this kenotic dimension. Excessive concern over the wearing of clerical attire or clerical forms of

---

23. *DMLPD*, #47.
24. Patrick McCaslin and Michael G. Lawler, *Sacrament of Service: A Vision of the Permanent Deacon Today* (New York/Mahwah, NJ: Paulist Press, 1986), 62–63.

address, or an attitude that certain ministries may be "theirs" by right of ordination may be signs in opposition to the kenotic nature of the diaconate.

Point #4: *The* ad intra *and* ad extra *methodology of Vatican II can assist in the development of theologies of ministry.*

At the suggestion of Cardinal Leon-Josef Suenens of Belgium, Pope John XXIII decided that the council's work would examine the church both *ad intra* and *ad extra*. This balanced approach helped the council fathers focus not only on the internal structures of the church, but on the church's relationships and mission as well.

Applying this approach to the nature of the diaconate within the constellation of ministries would seem to be a necessary and helpful dimension of theological activity. Ultimately, the meaning of diaconal ordination is not found only within itself, but only in its relationship with others. As theologian Edward Kilmartin once wrote: "Ministries of the Church must be consistent with the nature of the Church, or more precisely, derived from the nature of the Church. The way in which one conceives the nature of Church determines whether a particular form of ministry is acceptable."[25] Much of the decision to renew the diaconate as a permanent order

---

25. Edward J. Kilmartin, SJ, "Lay Participation in the Apostolate of the Hierarchy," in *Official Ministry in a New Age,* ed. James H. Provost (Washington, DC: CLSA, 1981), 94.

of the hierarchy came from a recovery of an ancient notion by many of the bishops at the council that the church herself was diaconal. Such a renewed emphasis on the diakonia of the church supported the renewal of a permanent order that sacramentalizes that diakonia. The renewed diaconate, therefore, is "derived from the nature of the Church."

John Paul II, in his 1987 address to the diaconate community gathered in Detroit made the following observation: "The service of the deacon is the Church's service sacramentalized. Yours is not just one ministry among others, but it is truly meant to be, as Paul VI described it, a 'driving force' for the Church's *diakonia*. You are meant to be living signs of the servanthood of Christ's Church."[26]

The challenge for theology, of course, is to develop a theology of diaconate that is consistent with, and respectful of, the sacramental identity and legitimate ministries of all other persons. When theologians consider the sacramental meaning of the deacon's ordination, they must do so in concert with the sacramental meaning of initiation as well as the sacramental meaning of presbyteral and episcopal ordinations. Conversely, when theologians distinguish the sacramental meanings of lay ministry, lay ecclesial ministry, and the ordained ministries of priests and bishops, they must do so without ignoring, minimizing, or doing violence to the sacramental meaning of diaconal ordination.

---

26. John Paul II, "Allocution to the Permanent Deacons and their Wives Given at Detroit, MI (19 September 1987)," *Origins* 17 (1987): 327–9.

Point #5: The permanence of the diaconate is at the core of the deacon's identity.

Despite often facile statements to the contrary, the diaconate never disappeared from the ordained ministries of the church. From the earliest scriptural references to the diaconate in the letters of St. Paul through today, the church has had deacons. What has happened, of course, is that the *way* in which the diaconate has been exercised has changed over the centuries. When the Second Vatican Council spoke of the diaconate, it focused on its renewal, revival, and restoration as a *permanent* order, in contrast to the *transitional* order it had become. In other words, the emphasis by the council was less on the renewal than it was on the permanence of the order. Expressed differently, it might be said that what was restored was the *permanence* of the diaconate, not the diaconate itself.

This newfound permanence was in sharp, and I would submit, radical contrast to the practice of more than a millennium, in which all ordinations were transitional, leading inexorably to the pinnacle of presbyteral ordination. Many theologians, including Thomas Aquinas, saw no sacramental significance to a bishop's ordination, seeing the bishop primarily as a priest who had received greater administrative jurisdiction. In the 1917 Pio-Benedictine *Code of Canon Law*, for example, we read that "first tonsure and orders are to be conferred only on those who are proposed for ascending to the presbyterate and who seem correctly understood as, at some point in the future, being worthy priests."

Vatican II deliberately reversed this practice, reclaiming the proper sacramental identity of the deacon's and the bishop's ordination and, in the case of the deacon at least, permitting this state of life to be exercised in a permanent way. The sacramental configuration of the deacon to Christ the Servant is a permanent effect of ordination.

It is for this reason that the subject of retaining the transitional diaconate continues to be a matter of significance in theological discourse. The maintenance of a transitional order of ministry seems to be contradicted by the council's decisions concerning tonsure, the minor orders, the subdiaconate, and the restoration of the permanency of the diaconate. The only sacramental vestiges of the *cursus honorum* rest with those deacons who transition into the presbyterate, and those presbyters who transition into the episcopate. The use of one sacramental order as a necessary prerequisite to another is a pattern that, at a minimum, is no longer absolute, and should be most closely examined. This is especially true if the sacramental potential of the renewed permanent diaconate is to be realized. The very permanence of the order of deacons lies at the theological core of the deacon's sacramental identity and ministry.

Point #6: Theologies of diaconate must recognize the unique sacramental relationship between the deacon and the bishop.

Vatican II reminds us that the bishop is the head of the diocesan church. It is the bishop who by virtue of his ordination has the fullness of responsibility for the diakonia of word, sacrament, and charity in the church. The bishop is the chief teacher, the chief liturgist as well as the "father of the poor." It is the bishop who, in the words of Susan Woods, Richard Gaillardetz, and others, "orders" ministry in the church. He appoints, installs, commissions, and ordains members of the diocesan church for service.

In a particular sacramental way, the deacon has his own unique relationship with the bishop. From the earliest scriptural references to the diaconate and throughout its "Golden Age," the deacon and his exercise of ministry have been linked to that of the bishop. This unique relationship continues to be stressed in contemporary magisterial documents. Liturgically it is expressed most significantly when, during the ordination of a deacon, only the bishop lays hands on the ordinand, contrasted with the ordination of presbyters and bishops, where all the members of those orders lay hands on the ordinands. The deacon, from the moment of ordination, is "ordered" to a participation in the bishop's own ministry. On certain occasions, some bishops continue to wear the deacon's dalmatic under their chasubles, again as a sign of their own diaconal responsibilities.

Helmut Hoping has written: "The presbyter represents the bishop *in situ,* that is, in the parishes, where they have governance of the parishes to which they have been assigned, and where they are responsible for presiding at the Eucharist....The deacon also has a share of the apostolic mission of the bishop. The deacon represents the bishop *in situ* in *diakonia,* which...is at the direct disposal of the bishop.[27]

One often rightly hears of the special sacramental and sacerdotal relationship that bonds the bishop with his body of priests. One should also hear of an analogous sacramental and diaconal relationship that bonds the bishop—the chief deacon of the diocese—with his body of deacons.

Point #7: The diaconate renewed by the Second Vatican Council is not simply a restoration of the ancient diaconate.

The contemporary diaconate is a new expression of this ancient ministry in the church. It is important to examine how this particular ministry relates to other ministries in the church. This renewed incarnation of the diaconate has emerged in a century of extraordinary social, economic, and political upheaval, and during a time of rapid, and some would say explosive, growth in lay ministry, coupled with a drastic decline in the number of presbyters. In light of these factors, it is important to discern the proper areas of ministry for the diaconate, so that it does not develop into a kind of substitute for sacerdotal ministry on the one hand or a

27. Helmut Hoping, "Diakonie als Aufgabe des kirchlichen Leitungsamtes," *Dokumentation 13—Jahrestagung 1996* (Tübingen: Arbeitsgemeinschaft Ständiger Diakonat, Bundesrepublik Deutschland, 1996), 34.

clericalized form of lay ministry on the other. The *Directory for the Ministry and Life of Permanent Deacons* states:

> In every case it is important, however, that deacons fully exercise their ministry, in preaching, in the liturgy and in charity to the extent that circumstances permit. They should not be relegated to marginal duties, be made merely to act as substitutes, nor discharge duties normally entrusted to non-ordained members of the faithful. Only in this way will the true identity of permanent deacons as ministers of Christ become apparent and the impression avoided that deacons are simply lay people particularly involved in the life of the Church.[28]

While a study of the scriptural and patristic evidence is important to an understanding of the diversity of function exercised by the ancient diaconate, it is critical to emphasize that the contemporary diaconate exists in a different set of cultural, geographical, political, and ecclesial realities. What history shows is an order flexible in its exercise and adaptable to a variety of pastoral situations; this makes the diaconate an order pregnant with potential in meeting contemporary needs. It would be unfortunate to attempt a rigid restoration of the ancient diaconate and thereby lose its inherent freedom for ministerial response. The contemporary diaconate is

---

28. Congregation for the Clergy, *Directory for the Ministry and Life of Permanent Deacons* (Vatican City: Libreria Editrice Vaticana, 1998), #40.

grounded on the balanced exercise of the threefold ministry; it is precisely in this balanced exercise that the deacon serves as a sacrament of unity, living through his ministry and life, the marriage of witness to Christ, the praise of God, and the care of neighbor. Christian discipleship demands *martyria, leitourgia,* and *diakonia:* The deacon serves as a public and permanent icon of the unity binding these three dimensions together. His particular role is to remind the church of its own sacramentality, of its own diakonia, of the church's responsibility to be a "sign and instrument" and "leaven and soul" in creating a more just world.[29]

Point #8: The renewal of the diaconate must be understood within the broader context of reform and renewal.

In the nineteenth century the first stirrings of a renewed diaconate rippled through Germany. This was not an isolated movement for enhanced works of charity; rather, it was part of an overall movement of renewal as the church attempted to discover its relationship to the modern world. This contextualized proposal for the renewed diaconate was further developed following Dachau and the Second World War, and may be seen in the discussions of Vatican II. In the ongoing development of the contemporary diaconate, it is necessary to consider the diaconate within this broader context. In certain areas, the diaconate is perceived as a movement in opposition

---

29. *Lumen gentium* 1; *Gaudium et spes* 40.

to reform and renewal, perpetuating an ancient, now-antiquated hierarchical order. As experience with the renewed diaconate continues, this context of reform and renewal will need to be developed: As the church continues to find creative ways to meet the needs of an increasingly complex world, she will need all of her resources, and the diaconate is one of those instruments of renewal. The diaconate recognizes the heritage of the church's tradition in light of living faith and the constant presence and action of the Spirit.

Point #9: *The deacon's ministry of word, sacrament, and charity is a function of leadership across the full spectrum of the triple* munus *of word, sacrament, and charity.*

The entire diaconal ministry revolves around pastoral leadership, not in terms of positional authority resulting from a participation in the bishop's own *episkopē* (for example, offices such as diocesan bishop, vicar general, or pastor), but in the sense of leading, inspiring, enabling, and modeling for other members of the church what servant-leadership can mean in living the demands of Christian discipleship in the contemporary world. The question of the relationship of the *episkopē* that characterizes the sacerdotal orders of bishop and presbyter to other forms of pastoral leadership demands critical examination that goes far beyond the scope of this presentation. Similarly, the question of how the deacon, who participates in a unique, nonsacerdotal way in the pastoral ministry of the bishop, might share in the bishop's *episkopē*, is also unresolved and in need of further explication. However, it may at least be said that the deacon is a leader within the community; the deacon, who receives no unique "power of order," is nonetheless empowered to be an icon of Christ the Servant: to speak and act in the name of Christ and of the church. Leadership is a baptismal charism, to be exercised in some way by all; leadership affirmed by ordination is leadership recognized permanently and publicly for the good of the church. Nathan Mitchell has written:

> By restoring the diaconate as a permanent role with the church's ordained leadership, Paul VI implicitly broke the long-standing connection between ordination and "sacramental power."…Theirs is a ministry, rooted like all others in a recognition of baptismal charism, that places pastoral leadership before sacramental power. The diaconate represents, then, those New Testament qualities of ministry which Schillebeeckx has aptly described as "the apostolic building up of the community through preaching, admonition and leadership." The restoration of the diaconate is thus important not because it resurrects an ancient order that had all but faded in the West, but because it affirms the principle that *recognition of pastoral leadership is the fundamental basis for calling a Christian to ordained ministry.*[30] [Emphasis in the original.]

Since the deacon's ministry is a participation in the bishop's own diakonia of word, sacrament, and charity, and with his public responsibility for the community, the deacon can make others aware of connection between faith and life. "In his ministry of the altar, he lays the needs of human beings on the eucharistic table, and naturally he also speaks of these needs when he preaches. He must make the parish aware of urgent situations of need, motivating them to share with one another and to give practical help."[31]

Point #10: Theologies of the diaconate must explore the untapped potential of expanded diaconal ministry, while avoiding the dangers of functionalism, to which it is particularly susceptible.

In years past, the ordination of priests and bishops spoke of the communication of powers to be exercised by the newly ordained. For example, the ordination of the presbyter conferred the power to offer the sacrifice of the Mass, and the ordination of the bishop conferred the power to ordain. This led in some circles to the unfortunate tendency to understand ordination as simply the transference of unique powers to the ordinands. One is only ordained a deacon for about two minutes before someone asks, "What do

---

30. Nathan Mitchell, OSB, *Mission and Ministry: History and Theology in the Sacrament of Order* (Wilmington, DE: Michael Glazier, Inc., 1982), 304.

31. Kasper, 40.

you do that priests do?" or, "What can you do that a layperson cannot do?" One wife of a deacon was once asked, "After you die, will your husband become a real priest?" Most deacons and their wives have similar stories.

This tendency to a functional approach to the diaconate is both a challenge and an opportunity. Since the deacon shares so many ordinary ministerial functions with presbyters, bishops, and laypersons, the challenge seems to be to find unique diaconal functions as if this will somehow justify the need for the diaconate in the first place. Some bishops, theologians, and parishioners have a sense that if there are no such unique diaconal functions, there is no need for the sacramental diaconate.

However, the shared functionality of the diaconate opens doors for an opportunity of a more profound understanding of sacramental ordination, an understanding that rightly focuses on the sacramental significance of the order as prior to its specific functions. Just as it is well accepted and understood that a proper sacramental understanding of the priesthood lies far beyond a simple listing of a priest's faculties, or that the sacramental understanding of matrimony extends far beyond the listing of a couple's daily activities, so too being a deacon is much more than a simple list of diaconal functions.

How might the deacon, as a sacramental sign of Christ's own kenosis, and as an official minister of the church's diakonia on behalf of his bishop, function in a way that extends this sacramental identity in practical ways?

Cardinal Walter Kasper has given us much food for thought in his own reflections on the diaconate. For example, he writes that the basic attitude of the deacon must "include a perceptive eye for those suffering distress, illness, or fear. The task is to bring a healing that sets free and empowers them to trust and so to serve and love others in their turn."[32] Furthermore, he challenges deacons to go beyond the provision of simple menial service alone; rather, "the goal of diaconal activity is not simply help, but the empowering of life, so that those who lie prostrate may get to their feet....In some situations, the deacon can and must become the public advocate of the weak and powerless and of all those who have no other voice or lobby."[33]

Much of Cardinal Kasper's work echoes the vision of the German researchers into the diaconate prior to Vatican II. Those researchers saw the deacon as the bishop's envoy to the most in need. Dedicated to building up the community in the name of the bishop, the deacon would have a very public identity as well as a commensurate responsibility for preaching in the midst of the assembly. This diaconal preaching was to stir up the fires of the community's own diakonia. Cardinal Kasper describes the deacon as the obvious and public "contact partner" for all those in need, to whom they know they can look confidently for help. As the official representative of

32. Kasper, 40.
33. Ibid.

the community, he is the obvious contact person for regional Catholic charity organizations and health centers.

The parish-based ministry of the deacon is extremely important in Kasper's view. He echoes McCaslin and Lawler when he suggests that it would be a good idea to provide at least one deacon for every parish so that the sacramental nature of the parish might be complete. He writes:

> Each parish has to make sure that *diakonia* is realized. This means that faith and preaching, as well as the Eucharist and liturgy must be oriented to *diakonia*. Faith without *diakonia* is not a Christian faith. Preaching without *diakonia* is not Christian preaching. A non-diaconal parish celebrating the Eucharist may express its faith, but its faith remains dead; in the final analysis it cannot find God, as they miss the point that God reveals himself in the people, especially in the poor.[34]

One of Cardinal Kasper's other ideas is already finding increasing support here in the United States. While the deacon may most frequently be assigned to parish ministry, Kasper writes that deacons should also be considered for assignments with an even broader scope—of city, deanery, and region. In the last national study on the diaconate, alluded to earlier, one of the principle findings was that while deacons have been well received in parish-based ministry, one

---

34. Kasper, 23.

of the primary challenges for the future would be "to broaden its ministries in order to be model, animator and facilitator of charity and justice" within the diocesan church.[35] To this end, many bishops now give their deacons a dual assignment: one to a parish and another to a diocesan or regional institution for service.

Kasper writes:

> I am thinking here of hospitals, homes for the elderly, spiritual care in places of work, in prisons, in refugee shelters, etc. I also include co-operation in the leadership of a diocese in those regions, where the main question is that of diaconal leadership. In this context, I would like to point out that for the bishop the community of deacons of a diocese can be a welcome panel of advisors. The deacons can act as the eyes and ears of the bishop in identifying areas of need and can help him in his task of being father to the poor.[36]

Such a vision restores some of the ancient responsibilities of the deacon, and the challenges it embodies would be profound, especially in the formation of deacons. Increasingly, ministries involving health care, prisons, and other areas of social concern are becoming more specialized, with stringent

---

35. United States Catholic Conference (USCC), *A National Study on the Permanent Diaconate of the Catholic Church in the United States, 1994–1995* (Washington, DC: USCC, 1996), 13.

36. Kasper, 27.

professional standards for their practitioners. Deacons assuming leadership roles in such areas will not only need the personal gifts and talents to serve in these areas, but will often need diocesan support to attain the appropriate professional credentials to enable their participation in them.

Finally, at the even broader level of more regional, national, and international ministries, one may turn again to the *Directory for the Ministry and Life of Deacons:* "A deeply felt need in the decision to re-establish the permanent diaconate was and is that of greater and more direct presence of Church ministers in the various spheres of the family, work, school, etc., in addition to existing pastoral structures."[37]

Deacons can and should exercise leadership in community-based service initiatives. Such service can take many forms, defined by the deacon's own skills and qualifications, the sociopolitical structures of the society in which he lives, and the needs to be met.

Furthermore, in terms of canon law, the deacon is the *only* cleric who may participate in various offices of public life, always with the permission of his bishop. While canon 285.3 prohibits clerics from assuming "public offices which entail a participation in the exercise of civil power," canon 288 exempts permanent deacons from this and other canons. While this does not exhaust the possibilities of community-based ministry, it remains largely unexamined.

---

37. John Paul II, catechesis at the General Audience of 6 October 1993, *Deacons Serve the Kingdom of God,* #6, in *Insegnamenti* XVI, 2 (1993), 954.

While precise data are unavailable, some deacons are serving as judges in civil and criminal courts, elected members of local governments, and even serving in positions of military authority. Such participation by deacons in offices of public life is unexplored territory for many reasons. Certainly there is concern that some forms of public life may be inappropriate for an ordained minister. Still another factor is the risk that the level of public scrutiny on the lives of its officials may be detrimental to the deacon and his role in the church. For these and similar reasons, the participation of a deacon in offices of public life is often an extraordinary, ad hoc matter between the deacon and his bishop. Nonetheless,

> It must not be forgotten that the object of Christ's *diakonia* is mankind. Every human being carries the traces of sin but is called to communion with God. "God so loved the world that He gave His only Son, so that all who believe in Him might not die but have eternal life" (John 3:16). It was for this plan of love that Christ became a slave and took human flesh. The Church continues to be the sign and instrument of that *diakonia* in history....Growth in imitation of Christ's love for mankind—which surpasses all ideologies—is thus an essential component of the spiritual life of every deacon.[38]

---

38. *DMLPD*, #49.

How the deacon, as a minister of the church in the world and as a leader in the church's diakonia, may best carry out these responsibilities in community-based ministries is an area that needs much greater examination. Opportunities for such service ought to be the subject of intense and intentional scrutiny by bishops, deacons, and those responsible for the formation of deacons.

Conclusion

It has been said that the Second Vatican Council did not restore the permanent diaconate because of a shortage of presbyters, but because of a shortage of deacons. Not surprisingly, Cardinal Kasper concurs when he observes that "we frequently hear about the 'shortage of priests' but I have yet to hear anyone lament the 'shortage of deacons.'"[39] Perhaps as we close these reflections, we may again take some inspiration from Professor Kerkvoorde:

Let us return once more to our diaconate that tiny light, which has stood all too long beneath the basket but, fortunately, has not yet been extinguished! Could not theology see a very beautiful, very fitting, and—for the Church and for the world—a very beneficial task for itself in pointing out the greatness of this simple service of living

39. Kasper, 37.

love of neighbor?... Theology could also facilitate the work of its restoration by not strangling it in a chaos of scholastic and legal terminology; by not constraining its unfolding right at the outset with emphasis on the danger of a possible deviation from true teaching or moral apprehensions; by not allowing this divine matter to be subordinated to the rights of human or ecclesiastical institutions; by clearing away all those outdated impediments that, while valid in their day, are no longer significant today; by emphasizing contemporary viewpoints of a service that fosters interpersonal contact between the faithful and pastors and sees therein the possibilities for building up a Christian community. Finally, [theology can] connect this sacramental significance to the words, example, and mission of Him, who said, "I did not come to be served, but to serve."[40]

---

40. Kerkvoorde, 138.

On the Theological Integrity of the Diaconate

Richard R. Gaillardetz, PhD
Murray/Bacik Professor of Catholic Studies
University of Toledo

Ministry is not an abstraction. Ministry is exercised by people and within relationships that are always situated in a particular place and a particular time. Terms like *priest, deacon, bishop,* and *lay minister* should not be treated as if they were Platonic ideals, as if there were an essential definition of each ministry. It is true that the Catholic Church's teaching office offers a set of doctrinal teachings that say something about ministry in general and ordained ministry in particular, but these are surprisingly sparse and serve more as survey lines that map out the boundaries of the faith, leaving considerable theological and pastoral territory within which to roam. One area in which there is still considerable room for exploration concerns a theology of the diaconate.

The status of the diaconate today is remarkably like that of lay ecclesial ministry: Both are largely postconciliar realities with ancient church roots. Both, in their contemporary forms, have grown at a rate that has outpaced theological reflection. I am not sure that we can adequately understand one without the other. In a recent review of literature on the diaconate, William Ditewig described the current pastoral theological context for the diaconate in terms of a "confluence of three realities": (1) the growth of lay ecclesial ministry in the decades since the council, (2) the restoration of the diaconate as a permanent and stable ministry, and (3) the decline in the numbers of presbyters.[1] We stand today at the pastoral and theological "delta" of this confluence, seeking to develop a theology of the diaconate that is faithful to our tradition and responsive to the needs of the moment.

An adequate theology of the diaconate today must meet four essential criteria: (1) It must do justice to the tradition of the church regarding the historical ministry of the diaconate, (2) it must explain why the diaconate is properly an ordained ministry, (3) it must distinguish the ordained ministry of the deacon from that of the presbyter and bishop, and (4) it must distinguish the ministry of the deacon from the ministry of the lay ecclesial minister without in any way denigrating the importance of lay ecclesial ministry. In this essay I wish to briefly consider three approaches to a theology of the diaconate often articulated in our present church setting. I will

---

1. William Ditewig, "The Once and Future Diaconate: Notes from the Past, Possibilities for the Future," *Church* 20 (Summer 2004): 51–54.

then sketch the outlines of a constructive theology of the diaconate that attempts to meet the four criteria I just mentioned.

Inadequate Approaches to a Theology
of the Diaconate

Contemporary pastoral practice, current diaconal formation programs, and recent ecclesiastical documents[2] all
give evidence of a startling diversity of theological understandings of the diaconate. In this section I will evaluate
three such theological approaches that I believe are defective
in some way.

The Cursus Honorum *and the Diaconate as Pastoral Internship for the Presbyterate*

By the end of the second century, the ministries of
bishop, presbyter, and deacon had developed as stable, distinctive "orders" in the church subject to sacramental ordination. In the Middle Ages, as the basic distinction between
the clergy and the laity became more pronounced, these
sacramental "orders" were hierarchically configured, along
with a number of other "minor orders" into what came to be
known as the *cursus honorum.* Not all ordained ministers

---

2. See the documents published by the Congregation for Catholic
Education and the Congregation for the Clergy: *Basic Norms for the
Formation of Permanent Deacons* and *Directory for the Ministry and Life
of Permanent Deacons* (Washington, DC: USCCB, 1998).

ascended this hierarchical ladder; we know of deacons like Francis of Assisi who remained deacons throughout their life. Nevertheless, the dominant ministerial path, particularly for diocesan clergy, was one in which the minister was expected to ascend the ministerial ranks, culminating in ordination to the priesthood. In the church of Rome this *cursus honorum* took the following form: porter, lector, exorcist, acolyte (the minor orders), followed by subdeacon, deacon, presbyter, and bishop (the major orders).[3] Over time the diaconate gradually lost its status as a stable, integral ministry of the church and was gradually reduced to a stepping-stone on the way to presbyteral ordination. Even after Pope Paul VI suppressed the minor orders, established the installed ministries of lector and acolyte, and restored the diaconate as a permanent and stable ministry, the diaconate has continued to function as a pastoral internship to be undertaken by a seminarian for between six and eighteen months as a preparation for presbyteral ministry.

This situation has required, at least from a canonical perspective, two different diaconates, one permanent and one transitional, with two different sets of canonical rights and obligations.[4] It is a situation that has served only to perpetuate

---

3. David Power, "Church Order," in *The New Dictionary of Sacramental Worship* (Collegeville, MN: The Liturgical Press, 1990), 216. For further studies into the history and contemporary significance of the "minor orders" see Winfried Haunerland, "The Heirs of the Clergy? The New Pastoral Ministries and the Reform of the Minor Orders," *Worship* 75 (July 2001): 305–20.

4. John Huels, "Special Questions on the Diaconate," *Liturgical Ministry* 13 (Winter 2004): 1–9 at 7–8.

a confused theology of the diaconate. Consequently, I am in sympathy with the proposal of Susan Wood that the church consider abandoning a transitional diaconate as a sacramental prerequisite to presbyteral ordination.[5] The reasons for this are many.

First, the ancient tradition in no way presupposed that one must advance from one ordained ministry to the next. In the earliest centuries, bishops were chosen both from the ranks of the baptized and from the diaconate without having to be first ordained presbyter. The most recent scholarship now suggests that a fixed sequence of ordination—deacon, presbyter, bishop—was not firmly in place before the Middle Ages.[6] Second, the existence of a "transitional diaconate" risks denigrating diaconal ministry by reducing it to a kind of pastoral internship or field education assignment. Third, although seminarians clearly benefit from a

5. Susan K. Wood, *Sacramental Orders* (Collegeville, MN: The Liturgical Press, 2000), 166–71. Huels believes that such a move could be justified as a means of removing canonical discrepancies. See Huels, 8.

6. See Wood's discussion in *Sacramental Orders,* 167. For recent research on the topic, see John St. H. Gibaut, *The Cursus Honorum: A Study of the Origins and Evolution of Sequential Ordination* (New York: P. Lang, 2000); Louis Weil, "Aspects of the Issue of *Per Saltem* Ordination: An Anglican Perspective," in *Rule of Prayer, Rule of Faith: Essays in Honor of Aidan Kavanagh, O.S.B.,* eds. Nathan Mitchell and John F. Baldovin (Collegeville, MN: The Liturgical Press, 1996), 200–17; Balthasar Fischer, "Hat Ambrosius von Mailand in der Woche zwischen seiner Taufe und seiner Bischofskonsekration andere Weihe empfangen?" in *Kyriakon* [Festschrift for Johannes Quasten], vol. 2, eds. Patrick Granfield and Josef A. Jungmann (Münster/Westfalem: Aschendorff, 1970), 527–31; Ormonde Plater, "Direct Ordination: The Historical Evidence," *Open* 37 (1992): 1–3.

pastoral internship that includes preaching and limited sacramental/liturgical ministry, there is no reason that these ministries could not be delegated to seminarians by their bishop without diaconal ordination.[7]

The Deacon as Icon of Christ the Servant

A second theological dead end attempts to develop a theology of the diaconate on the basis of the distinctive ministries and/or functions proper to the deacon. Building on common New Testament understandings of *diakonia,* many today try to ground the diaconate in the ministry of humble service.[8] This approach seems to have been foremost in the minds of the important leaders in the 1940s and 1950s who advocated the restoration of the diaconate. It continues to be influential in contemporary theologies of the diaconate. So, for example, Susan Wood describes the deacon as a sacramental icon of "the Servant Jesus who washed the feet of the apostles."[9] In this theological trajectory, diaconal ministry is

---

7. However, it should be noted that *Redemptionis sacramentum,* recently published by the Congregation for Divine Worship and the Sacraments, has prohibited even seminarians from preaching in the context of the Eucharist. *Origins* 33 (May 6, 2004): 801–22, see #66.

8. Hervé Legrand, "Le diaconat dans sa relation à la théologie de l'Église et des ministères," in *Diaconat, XXIe siècle. Actes du Colloque de Louvain-la-Neuve 13–15 septembre 1994,* eds. André Haquin and Philippe Weber (Brussels: Lumen Vitae, 1997), 13–41; Sherri L. Vallee, "The Restoration of the Permanent Diaconate: A Blending of Roles," *Worship* 77 (November 2003): 530–42.

9. Wood, 173.

often oriented toward ministry to the poor, the sick, the imprisoned, and all those who are marginalized. At present, variations on this particular theological trajectory seem to predominate in deacon formation programs. Yet, on closer examination this approach falters in important ways.

First, it is a weak theology that tries to ground any ministry in a purely functional description of what a minister does. Ministry is not just about what one does, but the character of one's relationship within the body of Christ. A theology of ministry must be grounded in ecclesial relationship, a claim that will be substantiated below. Second, the view of the deacon as icon of Christ the Servant can obscure the ways in which both the presbyter and bishop are no less called to lives of humble service than is the deacon.[10] Third, this approach founders historically because what we know of the ancient diaconate leads to the conclusion that diaconal ministry went far beyond ministries characterized as humble service to include preaching, catechesis, and management of the temporal goods of the church. Indeed, recent studies in the ancient diaconate suggest that there were precious few ministries of

---

10. The International Theological Commission seems to concur in this assessment: "[T]he ministries of the bishop and the priest, precisely in their function of presiding and or representing Christ the Head, Shepherd and Spouse of his Church, also render Christ the Servant visible, and require to be exercised as services. This is why it would seem problematic to aim to distinguish the diaconate through its exclusive representation of Christ as Servant, given that service should be considered a characteristic common to every ordained minister...." *From the Diakonia of Christ to the Diakonia of the Apostles* (London: Catholic Truth Society, 2003), 80.

the church that deacons did *not* undertake as proper to their vocation.

Finally, a more serious difficulty is presented by the recent scholarship regarding the biblical meaning of *diakonia*. In three important works,[11] John N. Collins has persuasively demonstrated that in the New Testament, diakonia never referred to humble service, to what we might call acts of Christian charity. According to Collins, the tendency to think of diakonia as a kind of Christian "social work" crept into Christianity by way of early twentieth-century German biblical scholarship. His careful philological analyses suggest that the root meaning of *diakonia* lies, not in humble service, but rather in one's having been sent or commissioned to fulfill the work or mandate of another. In this sense diakonia must be distinguished from ordinary Christian service to which all are called as followers of Christ.

Collins insists that in the New Testament, and particularly in the writings of St. Paul, *diakonia* describes a formal public ministry characterized by one's having been "sent" or "commissioned" on behalf of another. Thus, Collins's answer to the question that serves as the title of his second book, *Are All Christians Ministers?*, is, quite provocatively, "no." All Christians are certainly called to "service," that is, acts of

---

11. John N. Collins, *Diakonia: Re-interpreting the Ancient Sources* (New York: Oxford University Press, 1990); *Are All Christians Ministers?* (Collegeville, MN: The Liturgical Press, 1992); *Deacons and the Church: Making Connections Between Old and New* (Harrisburg, PA: Morehouse Publishing, 2002), 21.

Christian charity, but not all are called to formal ministry, or *diakonia,* in the church. Consequently, I think it is no longer acceptable to try to define the ministry of the deacon in terms of such service, as many have done in the past (including myself) by suggesting that the most appropriate ministry for the deacon is to be with the poor, the infirm, and the imprisoned. At the same time, I believe that some of Collins's conclusions may be overdrawn, and I agree with Professor Owen Cummings when he writes: "If service in terms of the diaconate is construed too narrowly, then Collins's strictures are well taken. But service in terms of building up the Church which, in turn, is building up the world toward greater and more aware communion with God is what not only the diaconate but the Church itself is all about."[12]

Perhaps Ditewig provides a way to reconceive the ministry of *diakonia* by configuring it not to menial service but rather to Christ's radical self-disposal or self-emptying, what the biblical tradition refers to as *kenosis.*[13] Here I think Ditewig has in mind a broad and theologically rich conception of service understood, not in terms of

---

12. Owen Cummings, "Theology of the Diaconate: State of the Question," *Proceedings 2004: Annual Convention and Business Meeting of the NADD* (2004): 21.

13. See William T. Ditewig, "Charting a Theology of Diaconate: An Exercise in Ecclesial Cartography," *Proceedings 2004: Annual Convention and Business Meeting of the NADD* (2004): 8–9. See also William T. Ditewig, "The Exercise of Governance by Deacons: A Theological and Canonical Study" (PhD Diss., Catholic University of America, 2002), 156–63.

functions or tasks, but rather in the unique way in which the deacon "empties himself" in a very concrete solidarity with the lives of ordinary believers, sharing with them many of their daily concerns for marriage, family, and profession. As theologically rich as this approach is, it does not seem to get at any attribute of diaconal ministry that is truly distinctive of the ministry and life of the deacon over against the universal demands of Christian discipleship.

Identifying the Distinctiveness of the Deacon in the "Clerical State"

Yet a third approach to the theology of the diaconate emphasizes the introduction of the deacon into the "clerical state." It should be remembered that diaconal ordination did not always mark the entry into the clerical state. For much of the second millennium, one became a cleric at tonsure, not at diaconal ordination. It was only with the directive of Pope Paul VI that minor orders were suppressed and two installed ministries, lector and acolyte, were created, that diaconal ordination came to effect introduction into the clerical state.[14]

The irony of this tendency to stress the deacon's participation in the clerical state is that, in many ways, it has been the restoration of the diaconate that has called into question

---

14. *Ministeria quaedam,* in *The Rites of the Catholic Church,* vol. 2 (New York: Pueblo, 1980).

the continued usefulness of the lay-clergy distinction.[15] The notion of the clerical state has for some time gone beyond a simple identification with holy orders to suggest a distinctive ontological identity reflected in a distinctive lifestyle. I am certainly not questioning the fact that diaconal ordination is a participation in the sacrament of holy orders, nor would I wish to deny that the deacon is, by ordination, newly configured within the life of the church and receives the sacramental character proper to ordination. I will say that, even granting the unique sacramental character that the deacon receives at ordination, there is a difference between one's being a "cleric" by virtue of ordination and one's belonging to a "clerical way of life," which the language of "clerical state" suggests. For a long time this distinction was moot because the clerical state was practically identified with celibacy in the Western Church. However, the restoration of the diaconate has made it possible for one to be a cleric while being married, and this not by way of canonical indult or dispensation but as an ordinary feature of diaconal ministry. Once we can speak of ordinary clerics as being married, having children, and pursuing a secular profession, it becomes difficult to see the continued helpfulness of speaking of a "clerical state" or a "clerical way of life" as distinct from a "lay state" or a "lay way of life."

Underlying this emphasis on the clerical state of the deacon are theological assumptions about the unity of the

---

15. See Richard R. Gaillardetz, "Shifting Meanings in the Lay-Clergy Distinction," *Irish Theological Quarterly* 64 (1999): 115–39.

sacrament of holy orders and a Western theology of the ontological change effected by ordination that only emerged in the second millennium. This shift in the understanding of ordination and ordained ministry in the second millennium was metaphysically underwritten by a substance ontology that attended primarily to those changes effected in a particular individual. This made it possible to identify ordained ministry in terms of the unique powers that were conferred through ordination. Many Western treatments of sacramental character have succumbed to the limitations of such a substance ontology, namely that it makes ontological claims regarding the individual abstracted from his or her relational existence within the life of the church. As I will suggest below, the language of ontological change can only be retained if it is transposed in a relational key in which attention is drawn, not to the isolated individual, but to the person-in-relation. Within such a relational ontology, the ontological change brought about by baptism, and the sacramental character thereby conferred, can only be appreciated adequately with respect to the ecclesial relationship constituted by baptism. In like manner, we can recognize a kind of ontological change effected in ordination that is oriented, not toward the conferral of powers on the ordinand, but toward the reconfiguration of the ordinand into a new ecclesial relation. The distinctive powers follow from the demands of this new ecclesial relation.

One possible consequence of grounding a theology of the diaconate in the deacon's identity as a cleric is that such an approach might suggest that the deacon participates, albeit in a subordinate degree, in the ministerial priesthood. This sacerdotal view of the diaconate, the deacon as "junior priest," has been used both to argue against the ordination of women to the diaconate and to justify the deacon's exercise of ministries that might seem more proper to the priest-presbyter. Because of growing shortages of priests in North America, many deacons are seeing their ministry filled with baptisms, weddings, and funerals, ministries that were once the province of the presbyter. The predominance of these exercises of diaconal ministry suggests a troubling shift in the ministerial shape of the diaconate today.[16] It may be canonically permissible and, in our present circumstances, even pastorally appropriate for deacons to preside over baptisms, weddings, and funerals, but sound ecclesiology and sacramental theology raises some questions. First, the preferred context for the celebration of baptism and the exchange of wedding vows is in the celebration of the Eucharist. This is because these sacraments, as sacraments of the church, ought to be celebrated before the larger Christian community and under the presidency of their pastor. The performance of baptism outside of the Sunday Eucharist, or the exchange of wedding vows outside the context of a nuptial Mass, ought to be seen as departures, however pastorally permissible, from the ecclesial and liturgical norm. Were pastoral practice of the church to enact more consistently the ideal of

---

16. See Richard R. Gaillardetz, "Are Deacons the Answer?" *Commonweal* 130 (August 15, 2003): 22–24.

baptisms performed at the Sunday Eucharist and the celebration of the nuptial Mass as the proper context for the exchange of marriage vows, the participation of deacons in both ritual actions would diminish. In many instances, deacons are exercising these ministries solely because of a shortage of presbyters. Such pastoral accommodations do not provide a solid foundation for a theology of the diaconate. Far better to develop a theology of the diaconate in that which is truly distinctive of the deacon's ministerial relationship within the church.

Finally, I believe this emphasis on the clerical status of the deacon has been used to justify deacons preaching in the context of the Eucharist while rejecting the possibility of lay preaching.[17] The theological rationale for both allowing diaconal preaching and excluding lay preaching is the status of the deacon as a "sacred minister." *Redemptionis sacramentum* acknowledges this when it states that "the homily on account of its importance and its nature is reserved to the Priest or Deacon during Mass."[18] I will argue below that the theological rationale for this situation is problematic.

Having indicated the inadequacy of each of these three approaches, let me turn now to develop a more constructive theology of the diaconate that fulfills the four criteria cited previously. However, an adequate theology of the diaconate

---

17. For the purposes of my argument, I am referring to preaching in the context of the Eucharist. I am aware that liturgical law does in fact allow for lay preaching in many other contexts.

18. *Redemptionis sacramentum*, #161.

cannot begin with the diaconate itself but must begin with a theology of ministry. And a theology of ministry, in turn, must begin with baptism.

Toward a Constructive Theology of the Diaconate

The documents of the council coined the term, *hierarchical communion.*[19] The term was developed, presumably, to forestall an understanding of ecclesial communion within the political framework of liberal democracy. However, the danger of continuing to use the language of "hierarchy" is that by describing the church as a *hierarchical* communion, you risk returning to the hierocratic, pyramidal view of the church that developed in the thirteenth century. That view, quite foreign to the first thousand years of Christianity, presented the church as a pyramidal structure in which the fullness of power *(plenitudo potestatis)* and truth was given to the pope and shared in diminishing degrees with the lower levels of church life.[20] Vestiges of this "trickle-down" view of hierarchy has remained, in spite of the council's reforms. Yet it is difficult to

19. The term appears five times in council documents (*LG* #21, 22; *CD* #4, 5; *PO* #7). It appears a sixth time in #2 of the *Nota praevia explicativa*. Walter Kasper offers a helpful discussion of the ambiguities surrounding this phrase in *Theology and Church* (New York: Crossroad, 1989), 156–61.

20. See Jean Leclerq, "Influence and Noninfluence of Dionysius in the Western Middle Ages," in *Pseudo-Dionysius: The Complete Works* (New York/Mahwah, NJ: Paulist Press, 1987), 31; Yves Congar, *L'Église de Saint Augustin à l'époque moderne* (Paris: Cerf, 1970), 229–30.

reconcile this view of hierarchy with the council's teaching about the fundamental equality of all the baptized, the universal call to holiness, and the nature of the church as the new people of God. If the language of "hierarchy" is to be redeemed, it must be purged of these pyramidal conceptions.[21] The church can be said to be hierarchical, not in the sense of a chain-of-command or a pyramidal structure, but in the sense that the church possesses a "sacred order" (hier-archē). The church then can be called "hierarchical" in the sense that it is an *ordered* communion constituted by a great diversity of ministries and Christian activities that together build up the life of the church.[22] This ordered communion is grounded in the sacrament of baptism.

Baptism and the Fundamental Ordering of the Church

Gerard Austin has referred to the early church's theology of baptism as the first Christian ecclesiology.[23] The early

---

21. For an attempt to retrieve the notion of "hierarchy" by distinguishing between "command hierarchy" and "participatory hierarchy," see Terence L. Nichols, That All May Be One: Hierarchy and Participation in the Church (Collegeville, MN: The Liturgical Press, 1997).

22. This view of the church as an ordered communion parallels in some ways Ghislain Lafont's presentation of the postconciliar church as a "structured communion." See his *Imagining the Catholic Church: Structured Communion in the Spirit* (Collegeville, MN: The Liturgical Press, 2000).

23. Gerard Austin, "Restoring Equilibrium After the Struggle with Heresy," in *Source and Summit: Commemorating Josef A. Jungmann, S.J.,* eds. Joanne M. Pierce and Michael Downey (Collegeville, MN: The Liturgical Press, 1999), 35–47 at 37.

Christians understood themselves to be forged, through faith and baptism, as a new people of God. For the author of 1 Peter, baptism was not a private action but rather an ecclesial act that inserted one into a "chosen race, a royal priesthood, a holy nation, God's own people" (1 Pet 2:9) where the priestly life of the community lay, not in any ritual action, but in the everyday holy living of the entire Christian community.

Paul certainly did not understand baptism to be a private religious event either; for Paul, baptism initiated the believer into the "one body" (1 Cor 12:13), the church. By baptism into the Christian community one participated in a new reality; one was a "new creation" (2 Cor 5:17; Gal 6:15). This new form of Christian living was given shape by the cross and resurrection of Christ (Rom 6:3–11), the "paschal mystery."

From a biblical perspective, we might say that Christian initiation "orders," or "configures" the believer to Christ *within* the community of faith, Christ's body. Baptism does not just make one a different kind of individual, it draws the believer into a profound ecclesial relationship, one's ecclesial *ordo* within the life of the church. One's personal identity is fully disclosed in the life of the church. Moreover, when we consider the sacraments of initiation as a unity, we recognize that initiation possesses its own anointing, "laying on of hands," and entrance into eucharistic communion. To be initiated into the church is to take one's place, one's *ordo* within the community of the baptized. As the influential Greek Orthodox theologian and metropolitan, John Zizioulas, puts it, "there is no such thing as non-ordained persons in the church."[24] To be baptized is to be "ordained" into our most basic ecclesial relationship as disciples of Jesus Christ.

The distinctive character of this baptismally ordered relationship unfolds in three dimensions. Vertically, if you will, we are baptized into communion with God, in Christ, by the power of the Spirit. Yet this relation is inseparable from our horizontal relationship with all our brothers and sisters in baptism who constitute together a communion of believers. These two dimensions of the baptismal ordering must, in turn, be conjoined to a third dimension, the movement outward in mission toward the world. This three-dimensional ecclesial relation established by Christian initiation offers us our primal identity as Christian believers and it can never be abandoned.

The theological status of the church as an ordered communion is exhibited in a most profound way in the celebration of the Eucharist. It is the whole community of the baptized, Christ's body, that is the subject of the eucharistic celebration, always under the necessary presidency of a priest or bishop and customarily assisted by the deacon. Yet in the Eucharist the entire assembly is drawn simultaneously into communion with God and with one another and it is the whole community that is sent forth from the Eucharist in mission into the world.

---

24. John D. Zizioulas, *Being as Communion: Studies in Personhood and the Church* (Crestwood, NY: St. Vladimir's Seminary Press, 1985), 215–6.

Ministry Within an Ordered Communion

It is this view of the church as an ordered communion of relationships grounded in baptism that provides the basis for our understanding of ministry. Ministry within the church is ordered in any number of ways. Some among the baptized are commissioned to engage in formal but more occasional ministries, like those of the catechist or the liturgical ministries of the lector or cantor. Others among the baptized function as what the American bishops have begun to refer to as lay ecclesial ministers, engaging in ministries that require significant formation and commitment. One thinks of the many professional lay ministers who work in Christian formation or youth ministry. What makes all of these actions ministries, properly speaking, is the way in which each of these ecclesial activities brings the Christian into a new, public, and formally accountable ecclesial relationship.

Finally, at least since the second century, the Church has called some from among the baptized to sacramental ordination as bishops, presbyters, or deacons. We hold that sacramental ordination ecclesially repositions the one being ordained into a new, permanent, and lifelong ecclesial relationship. James Puglisi's careful study of the ancient ordination rituals of the Western Church confirms this analysis.[25] What Puglisi's study suggests is that the early church's developing theology of ministry focused not on powers conferred, but on

---

25. James Puglisi, *The Process of Admission to Ordained Ministry: A Comparative Study* (Collegeville, MN: The Liturgical Press, 1996), I: 205.

the new ecclesial relationship into which the ordinand was configured. But how do we characterize each of these new ecclesial relationships constituted by ordination?

In the early church the privileged role of the bishop lay in his unique ministry of *episkopē,* the pastoral oversight of a eucharistic community in which the bishop functioned as the chief judge and witness to the apostolic faith, the servant of the unity of that community, and the agent for bringing that community into communion with other communities. By the third century, the presbyter gradually was given a share in this ministry of apostolic oversight, though limited to oversight of a particular community under the leadership of the bishop. Whether in the case of the bishop or later the presbyter, eucharistic presidency followed from their de facto pastoral leadership over a community.[26] Their ecclesial relationship to the local church was decisive. The empowerment for sacramental ministry was offered in view of their ecclesial relationship as leader of the community.

The diaconate presented a somewhat different situation because the deacon's sacramental relationship within the life of the church was not constituted by the ministry of apostolic oversight *(episkopē),* as with the bishop or local presbyter. However, and I take this to be decisive for understanding the diaconate, the deacon was ordained *to serve* the ministry of *episkopē.* In other words, the ministry of the deacon must be understood not in terms of powers conferred, nor by the

---

26. Hervé-Marie Legrand, "The Presidency of the Eucharist According to the Ancient Tradition," *Worship* 53 (1979): 407.

functions or particular ministries he performs, nor as icon of Christ the Servant, nor by his introduction into the clerical state, but by his public service to the apostolic ministry of *episkopē* exercised by the bishop or presbyter.

The Diaconate: In Service of the Ministry of Episkopē

For both the presbyter and bishop, ordination introduces them into a new relationship within the church characterized by pastoral oversight *(episkopē)* and ritualized, as it were, in their presidency at the celebration of the Eucharist.[27] This ministry of pastoral oversight is also called "apostolic" insofar as it is explicitly concerned with preserving the church's continuity in teaching and practice, with its apostolic origins. The deacon is also ordained into apostolic office, but his share in this office is not by way of *exercising* pastoral oversight (the ministerial province of the bishop and presbyter) properly speaking, but of *assisting or serving the needs of pastoral oversight* as determined by the one who exercises that oversight. Let me develop this more.

The research of John Collins suggests that diakonia had as its foundational biblical meaning the sense of being publicly commissioned or sent forth on behalf of another. Thus, the deacon is the one who is "sent forth" by the bishop (and at

---

27. I cannot address here the difficult question of how this theology relates to professed religious priests who may not exercise pastoral oversight of a particular community.

times, indirectly by the local pastor) in service of the needs of the church as seen by the one charged with oversight of the local church. It is true that all ministries, lay and ordained, are subject to the ordering of the bishop or pastor, but the ministry of the deacon is not only *ordered by* the one responsible for apostolic oversight, his ministry is explicitly *placed at the service of* that ministry of oversight. To test the adequacy of this theological approach to the diaconate, let us see whether it fulfills the four criteria for a theology of the diaconate.

A theology of the diaconate must do justice to the tradition.

As I noted earlier, the deacon of the early church exercised a broad range of ministries. We have early documentary testimony of the liturgical ministry of the deacon, of the ministry of preaching, the ministry to the sick, the administration of the temporal goods of the local church, and the ministry of catechesis. We have the historical witness of deacons who were accomplished theologians like Ephrem of Nisibis or later in the Middle Ages, of Alcuin of York.[28] In the midst of this great diversity in pastoral ministry, the most consistent feature of diaconal ministry seems to have been the deacon's distinctive relationship to the bishop. This is reflected in the ordination ritual for deacons found in Hippolytus's *Apostolic Tradition,* in which the deacon is ordained not into the priesthood but into "service of the bishop" *(in ministerio*

---

28. Cummings, "Theology of the Diaconate," 34–35.

episcopi).[29] The testimony of our tradition does appear to affirm that what distinguished the ancient diaconate was not what the deacon did or did not do, it was his commitment to be sent in service of the needs of the church as discerned by the one charged with apostolic oversight (the bishop).

> *A theology of the diaconate must explain*
> *why deacons should be ordained.*

One can recognize many different ministries in the church today, but not all of them are participations in an "apostolic office." It is the deacon's explicit service to the pastoral oversight of the bishop and presbyter that justifies his share in that apostolic office. Ordination does place the ordinand into a new ecclesial relationship. For deacons this new relationship is characterized by the unique bond between the deacon and bishop that is expressed in the formal promise of obedience that a deacon makes to his bishop. It is further expressed in the ancient Christian conviction that once having been sacramentally ordained within the church, one is never reordained. In other words, the early Christians soon

---

29. Bernard Botte, ed., *La tradition apostolique* [Sources chrétiennes, 11], (Paris: Cerf, 1984), chapter 8. It is certainly noteworthy that while *Lumen gentium* 29 draws on this formula, *non ad sacerdotium, sed ad ministerium,* it does not make any explicit reference to the clause found in the *Apostolic Tradition* regarding service to the bishop. This point was made by the ITC in their document as well, *From the Diakonia of Christ to the Diakonia of the Apostles,* 85.

recognized that such ministries placed one in a permanent, new relationship within the church. Finally, this close relationship to the one responsible for pastoral oversight is reflected in the way in which the deacon's liturgical ministry is visibly aligned with the one who presides over the church's worship. Within the worshipping assembly the vested deacon stands at the side of the liturgical presider who exercises liturgical *episkopē* He is blessed by the presider prior to his proclamation of the gospel, and he explicitly serves the ministry of the presider in the petition for God's mercy during the penitential rite, in the preparation and distribution of the eucharistic gifts, and in the call for the gathered assembly to share the peace of Christ.

A theology of the diaconate must distinguish diaconal ministry from that of the presbyter and bishop.

In the midst of the diverse ministerial activity that has characterized the work of deacons, it must be said that deacons did not ever, as an ordinary dimension of their ministry, exercise pastoral oversight of a local eucharistic community. That is not to say that deacons have never engaged in this ministry, merely that when they did so it was recognized as an exceptional accommodation to a shortage of presbyters. This then is the crucial distinction between the ministry of the deacon and that of the bishop and presbyter. According to church teaching, the presbyter and bishop are ordained to minister *in persona Christi capitis* ("in the person of Christ as head"), but not the deacon.[30] This phrasing does not, as the scholastic tradition sometimes suggested, refer exclusively or even primarily to the priest's cultic role in "confecting" the Eucharist, but rather to his acting in the person of Christ as head of the church, that is, as the minister charged with apostolic oversight of the local community.[31]

Deacons do not, as an ordinary dimension of their ministry, exercise this "headship" or apostolic oversight of a community. Note that I am intentionally using the term *oversight (episkopē)* rather than the broader term, *leadership*. It goes without saying that deacons are called, by virtue of their public ministry, to be leaders in the church. So too, in fact, are lay ecclesial ministers and others who have taken public roles in the church. Leadership can and does take many forms. I am arguing that it is only one very particular kind of pastoral leadership, *episkopē* or apostolic oversight, that in the Catholic tradition has been reserved to the bishop and presbyter.

It is for this reason that I have some concern regarding the growing practice of making training to serve as pastoral administrators an integral feature of diaconal formation pro-

---

30. For a history of the origin and usage of the *in persona Christi—in persona ecclesiae* schema, see Bernard D. Marliangeas, Clés pour une théologie du ministère: in persona Christi, in persona Ecclesiae (Paris: Éditions Beauchesne, 1978).

31. For a discussion of whether and to what extent the deacon might act *in persona Christi capitis,* see the ITC document *From the Diakonia of Christ to the Diakonia of the Apostles,* 77–79; Ditewig, "The Exercise of Governance by Deacons," 164–6.

grams. This training risks giving the impression that serving as a pastoral administrator is an "ordinary" ministry of the deacon. Although canon 517.2 stipulates that the deacon is to have precedence over the nonordained faithful in the delegation of pastoral responsibility over a parish without a priest-pastor, this does not change the fact that a responsibility for the exercise of *episkopē* is being delegated to the deacon that does not properly pertain to diaconal or, for that matter, lay ministry. The ministry of the deacon is no more oriented toward the actual exercise of apostolic oversight than is the ministry of the layperson. Both the deacon and the layperson, when serving as pastoral administrators, are engaged in what, from an ecclesiological point of view, must be considered extraordinary ministries proper to the presbyter. In the ancient church, the sacramental ministry of the presbyter developed precisely because, when a bishop could not personally exercise pastoral oversight of a eucharistic community, he sent a presbyter, not a deacon, to serve as an extension of the liturgical ministry of episkopē.

It is difficult to avoid the conclusion that it is our present canonical discipline, and not sound theology, that prevents us from pursuing what is clearly the most appropriate ecclesiological response to a situation in which a community is to be deprived of a presbyter for an extended period of time. That response would be to ordain the de facto pastoral leader of that community, whether they be deacon or layperson, to the order of presbyter, that is, to that ordained ministry the principal responsibility of which is to provide such apostolic oversight in communion with the bishop.

A theology of the diaconate must distinguish the diaconate from lay ecclesial ministry without diminishing lay ecclesial ministry.

Finally, I want to test this theology of the diaconate by considering it in relation to lay ecclesial ministry. I do so not just for reasons of theological consistency, but because in some pastoral settings the relationship between the deacon and the lay ecclesial minister has been tainted by resentment and misunderstanding. I have argued in other contexts that lay ecclesial ministry must be recognized as a public, ordered (not ordained) ministry in the church.[32] Every Christian possesses charisms to be exercised in their daily life. These charisms may appear quite ordinary (making them no less vital), such as the charism of parenting[33] or imbuing the atmosphere of one's workplace with the values of the gospel. At other times these charisms may take on a more dramatic and even public character, as in the evangelical witness of Dorothy Day. The exercise of these charisms, however

---

32. See Richard R. Gaillardetz, "The Ecclesial Foundations of Ministry Within an Ordered Communion," in *Ordering the Baptismal Priesthood*, ed. Susan K. Wood (Collegeville, MN: The Liturgical Press, 2003), 26–51.

33. See Wendy Wright, "The Charism of Parenting," in *Retrieving Charisms for the Twenty-First Century*, ed. Doris Donnelly (Collegeville, MN: The Liturgical Press, 1999), 85–101.

dramatic, does not call for undertaking any new ecclesial relationship for the sake of the church and its mission beyond that constituted by baptismal initiation. However, there are other charisms, the manifestation of which does suggest the suitability of entering into a new, public, ecclesial relationship within the church. So a local community might recognize in a particular candidate the charism of teaching, and call them into a new ministerial relationship within the church as a director of Christian formation. This new ministry ought properly to be ritualized by a corresponding rite of installation.

It will often be the case that the particular ministries engaged by deacons and those of lay ecclesial ministers (such as the director of Christian formation) will overlap considerably. Indeed, a case can be made that they ought to overlap even more than they do now. I have in mind the preaching ministry that, by church law, a deacon but not a layperson may exercise in the context of a homily offered within the celebration of the Eucharist. Since the deacon does not himself exercise the ministry of liturgical *episkopē*, his preaching ministry is by necessity engaged under the presidency of the bishop or presbyter presiding at that Eucharist. It is the bishop and/or the presbyter who *presides over* the ministry of the word. This is reflected in the deacon's reception of a blessing from the presider prior to the proclamation of the gospel and the offering of the homily. The deacon exercises the charism of preaching (and he should not be allowed to preach if he does not possess this charism)[34] under the presidency of the one who oversees the liturgical ministry of the word. Consequently, it is difficult for me to understand why a layperson might not also exercise the charism for preaching in the context of the Eucharist since they too would only be doing so under the presidency of the bishop or presbyter.

In any event, the overlap in the actual ministries performed by deacons and lay ecclesial ministers need not threaten the theological integrity of the diaconate. Deacons will often work side by side with lay ecclesial ministers in catechesis, youth ministry, peace and justice advocacy, or the administration of the business concerns of a parish or other Catholic institution. Their performance of these ministries will generally be, in substance, no different from that of lay ecclesial ministers. Moving in the other direction, it should be pointed out that many of the ministries often presented as distinctive to the deacon (for example, preaching, presiding at baptisms, weddings, and funerals) can, in extraordinary circumstances, be engaged by laypersons. What distinguishes the diaconate from lay ministry is not the substance of their ministerial activity, but the way in which what the deacon does is much more explicitly a function of his service to the directives of the bishop and/or the pastor. The deacon is "sent" by the bishop into a particular pastoral field. This does not mean that the deacon is unable to engage in genuine

---

34. The same should hold for the bishop and presbyter, of course, but that is an argument for another day.

pastoral initiative, but it does mean that his ministry is much more explicitly a function of his having been sent by the one with pastoral oversight. By virtue of his promise of obedience to the bishop and his lifelong commitment to diaconal ministry, a commitment the church does not require of lay ministers, the deacon serves explicitly in response to the needs of the community as discerned by the bishop or his pastor. This sense of the deacon being bound closely to the discerned needs of the bishop is reflected in the growing practice in many dioceses of deacons being assigned by the bishop to diaconal ministry in a parish other than the one in which their formation was first begun or in some extra-parochial ministry.

Lay ministry too may emerge from the pastoral initiative of the bishop/pastor, but it more often emerges from the recognized charisms of the laity and the grassroots discernment of the ministerial needs of the local community. There is a freedom for pastoral initiative, always subject to the ultimate ordering of the bishop or pastor, that I believe is more characteristic of lay ministry than it is of diaconal ministry.

Conclusion

In this essay I have tried to make a case for a new theology of the diaconate that is faithful to our tradition yet is responding to the unique circumstances of the church today. It is a ministry that possesses its own intelligibility without in any way threatening or calling into question the many other manifestations of the Spirit evident in the ministerial activity of the church. The restoration of the diaconate reminds the church that the essence of ministry does not lie in pursuing one's own pet projects and programs ("this is my ministry"). The diaconate teaches us that ministry does not lie in doing any particular thing at all, but rather in allowing oneself to be sent forth—by Christ, by the bishop, by the church—to embody in one's whole way of life that kenotic pattern of dying and rising, what we call the paschal mystery, which is the inner grammar of all Christian living.